IRIS

IRIS

by Mark Jarman

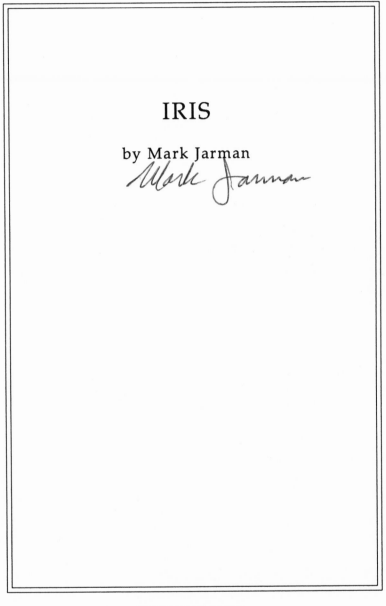

STORY LINE PRESS

1992

ISBN: 0-934257-88-4 (paper)
ISBN: 0-934257-87-6 (cloth)

This publication was made possible thanks in part to the generous support of the Nicholas Roerich Museum, the Andrew W. Mellon Foundation, and our individual contributors.

Book design by Lysa McDowell

The artist, Sara Rossberg, whose painting, "Blue in Yellow" appears on the front cover is represented by Rosenberg & Stiebel, Inc., New York.

Published by Story Line Press, Inc.
Three Oaks Farm in Brownsville, OR 97327

ACKNOWLEDGEMENTS

Passages from "The World's Wonders," "Morro Bay," and "The Eye" from SELECTED POETRY OF ROBINSON JEFFERS by Robinson Jeffers. Copyright 1941, 1944, 1951, 1952, by Robinson Jeffers and renewed 1969, 1972 by Donnan Jeffers and Garth Jeffers. Reprinted by permission of Random House, Inc.

The passage from "Tor House" from ROCK AND HAWK by Robinson Jeffers. Copyright 1928 and renewed 1956 by Robinson Jeffers. Reprinted by permission of Random House, Inc.

Grateful acknowledgment to Mrs. Donnan Jeffers for permission to adapt lines from the forward to JEFFERS COUNTRY by Una Jeffers.

The author also gratefully acknowledges the editors of The Hudson Review where part one of IRIS first appeared.

Special thanks are due to Virginia Schaefer.

For my mother

It is easy to know the beauty of inhuman things, sea,
    storm and mountain: it is their soul and their
    meaning.
Humanity has its lesser beauty, impure and painful;
    we have to harden our hearts to bear it.

I have hardened my heart only a little . . .

—Robinson Jeffers
"The World's Wonders"

I

The woman sat on the bus, her daughter's head in her lap,
and read a paperback of poems,
The only book from college that she'd saved, Robinson
Jeffers, and talked back to him,
As always. He was her poet. The bus crossed the two
lakes, and the land between them,
Like stages of warning. Glare of water, shadow of close,
dense trees, glare again.
Then entry into the isolated flatland that she'd left,
married, pregnant, unhurt,
Not yet in thrall to this dead stranger from California,
who spoke of an end to the continent
She had to imagine, had to summon up even more strenuously
while coming back
To western Kentucky, a mother, estranged, abused and wounded,
hiding a black-eye behind dark glasses.
Her daughter curled her legs on the hard vinyl seat. She
sucked her thumb and sighed for the trip to end.
The windbreak oaks dangled their pea-green April flowers; a
field flashed a green facet of winter wheat.
Iris read about granite and spray and poppies and said
to her poet, "What is a ground-swell?
Why do you envy hardness? My mama has gotten hard. Oh,
what will she say when she sees us?"

When Iris came home, she saw the new Chevy truck, with
camper top, and Hoy and Rice, her brothers,
Standing back to smell its newness, like part of the spring
air. Fat Hoy like a friar,
His black hair shining like a wallet with greaseless hair
oil. His twin, Rice, like the after-picture

From the diet ads, thin as a hoe handle, his hair, too,
  slick with the same stuff.
Their dachsund Crank, with L-shaped broken tail like a
  tire iron, looked up at them,
As if they were big dogs in charge of frolicking, and
  waited for the fun to start.
Iris and Ruth had hitched a ride from the Dairy Queen,
  across from the bus stop, and the ice cream
Ruth had eaten still haloed her mouth. Uncle Hoy grabbed
  her up and kissed it away.
And Rice, full of joy for his truck, took the cases out
  of his sister's hands, and took Iris into his arms.
She let him feel the skinny ribs and remove the sunglasses
  to see the nicotine stain
Of the healing black-eye, only part of the settlement
  from Cale. "Oh, Rice," she said, surprised
At her own joy in saying it, "we've had some real bad times."
  The dog Crank barked and frisked.
And there was the sound of Ruthie squealing as Hoy burred
  her neck with his fleshy lips.

Around them ploughed fields, windbreak trees, the bisecting
  road where, when traffic passed,
It was only a single truck with its rising and falling
  wind. Set on its dirt apron,
The mobile home almost looked permanent, brushed by
  the branch tips of two hedgeapple trees,
Male and female. Old trees to match, in Iris's mind,
  her poet's redwoods. Their flesh
Orange in the ruts of the bark, and the bark, soaked with
  spring rain, green near the root.

The corn would go in, the soybeans, and the tobacco. All
   of this was in the offing. Surely, these were labors
Her poet could approve of. High up the hedgeapples wore
   stiff thorns only birds and squirrels
Could pick among safely. She longed to climb up there
   for the hawk's view, the lofty gaze as if down on
   furrows of white surf.
Soon the sea around them would be the seasonal green,
   the dense eradication of space by flourishing growth.
"Nobody told me you was coming home," said Mama.
   The woman did a funny dance of ire or nervousness
Beside the steps, wandering in a tight circle, as if to
   wind herself up.
"I didn't tell nobody, Mama," Iris said. "I've got
   Ruthie here." Mama picked the child up
As if the mother had left her for an overnight. "Give
   your old grandma a kiss, then."
And offered her puffy cheek and grinned, the once beautiful
   smile now cracked and discolored.
Only a drunk's blurred vision could restore it. "Where's
   Cale, then?" Mama said.
She wouldn't look at Iris or at Ruth, though the child
   straddled her hip
And kneaded the smeared tattoo on her flabby upper arm
   and studied the smallpox dent.
"It was them drugs, wasn't it?" And Iris looked away, too.
   Hoy and Rice
Had boarded their new truck, full of seed bags, and would
   drive it out to the field's far edge.
"Drugs and that old woman, Mama. You know," Iris said,
   and again that odd joy

Seized her. "Poor Cale needed a Mama just like me. She
    gave him money, too."
"You know what your brothers is doing, don't you?" Mama
    put Ruthie down, gently, and the child
With nothing to occupy her stood between the two
    grown-ups and sucked her thumb.
Mama pointed out at the far edge, the windbreak there,
    where the truck's chrome sparked with reflected sun.
"Gonna plant us a nice cash crop of marijuana out there
    in the drainage ditches." Then, piously,
"Did it last year. Worked real well. But I don't want
    to see it in my house, you hear?
It's not like beer you know will get you hammered and make
    you pay next morning. It's the money.
We got to have the money. I don't want that Cale to know."
    Iris wept it—"Mama!"
And Ruthie gasped. Iris said, "He's not talked to me since
    he beat me up. He's with that woman
Down Chattanooga way." "Don't want it nowhere but out in
    that field," Mama said.
"In the drainage ditches near them red oaks. Don't want
    to see it. Don't want to know until we got the money."

Iris picked up the bags and one of his lines rose to mind
    with the simple motion of lifting them—
How her poet's place above the ocean like all beautiful
    places called for a sad story, a terrible
Event. That sounded to her like a wish no sane person
    would wish. She remembered his image
Of the roof below trees and a cornfield and a woman beating
    a horse, her son tying a chain to the horse's tongue.

You cannot live like that, she said to herself, and lugged
    the cases up the metal stairs,
Calling Ruth as if it were she in a revery, stopped and
    letting the world spin along.
Mama was making noise in the kitchen. Ruth held the dog;
    he licked the remaining sweetness off
Her face. The brief span of pleasure, a balm in the air,
    before the summer's green
Thickened and turned feverish and the great globes of useless
    fruit appeared in the hedgeapple and drummed
On the roof—a respite, but was it like the beaten horse's
    or like the woman's whose arm grew tired of punishment?

"This is Hoy's favorite," Mama said and poured macaroni
    shells into a pan at a rolling boil.
Its heat filled the kitchenette and dinette, the hamburger
    turned gray in the frying pan.
Ruth, thumb in mouth, stroking the dog, sat in the maroon
    overstuffed chair
Before the TV, the monster set that dwarfed the living
    area, shrunk further
By the cot for her bed and the suitcases open by the couch
    where Iris would sleep. All windows open,
All curtains passing breezes back and forth, the A/C
    unit, big as the TV,
Crouched silent in its window, waiting for summer, Hoy
    and Rice on the metal stairs
With beers and cigarettes. "I'll just pour this fat off,
    Mama," Iris said. "No!"
Mama grabbed the handle. "No," she said. "Hoy wants that
    on the noodles, instead of butter.

Rice likes it, too. I don't mind it myself. Get you that
   salt cellar and pepper there."
Meat and shells. And green beans from the can. Peaches
   from the can in their juice. Glasses of milk
For Hoy and Rice and Ruth, instant iced tea for Iris and
   Mama. "Didn't you set
That table, then?" Mama asked. "Teach that little girl
   to set this table. You'll both need
To do your chores." At dinner, Ruth asked Iris to pick
   the meat out of her shells,
The glistening mess of pieces of broken macaroni, wilted
   with overcooking, some few keeping
Their shapes to confirm that this was Hoy's favorite—
   doughy shells, lips closed, all greased with sweet fat.
They sat, the five of them, at the oblong formica table,
   with its ridged chrome side,
In padded plastic upholstered chairs on springy chrome
   legs turned in U's and S's.
All windows open, the light burning low behind the black
   hedge of red oaks.
Among the still naked branches of the hedgeapples, Iris
   pictured the stars,
The exiting winter constellations appearing face down
   toward the west, led by Orion
Into that low dull redness over the mobile home's
   aluminum roof.
Then the breeze, sipping in through the window by the table,
   took on a chill, making a shiver pass
Like a static electric shock through each of them, almost
   making them smile—Hoy, Rice, Iris.
Mama stood and, going window to window, struggled with the
   flimsy metal frames and forced each shut.

Iris undressed in the bathroom, among its gold flecks on
       white, like scrambled eggs, noticing
The galaxy of coal-black mildew across the shower's glass
       door, the cup of toothbrushes that,
When she knocked it over, showed a gummy residue that
       smelled rank. She washed it out.
Standing erect, she looked at herself, caught naked in
       the dingy glare. A boy with tits,
She recalled Cale laughing once, laughing because that must
       have been what he liked.
Having a baby had spread her hips a little, softened her
       belly slung above her pelvis,
And her small breasts hung, no longer alert and pointed,
       their nipples soft, oblong, indented.
She turned her right side to the mirror to check the bruise
       mapping upward from
Buttock to ribs, charting Cale's last kick. Hardly the
       heroine for you, she said to her poet.

It was the close community of sleepers Iris had come home
       for. Now she listened to them.
Hoy and Rice in their room off the hall sighed and farted
       as they fell asleep. In the master bedroom,
That balanced the metal rectangle, end of the hall, Mama
       murmured a man's name—her dead husband's?—
Woke herself, whispered, soon slept again, muttering something
       else.
Ruth lay like a four-limbed starfish on her camp cot,
       nightgown hiked up to her navel, unguarded.
Iris tucked her in. The dog Crank, tapping with unclipped
       nails across the kitchen linoleum,

Slurped water from his dish, sleepwalked back to Hoy and
   Rice. Soon Iris, too,
Would be part of this, as she needed to be. The lamp,
   set on a TV tray, she turned on dim
And took the paperback from her purse, the book already
   beginning to be worn from reading.
She looked at the poet's face on the cover, the charcoal
   angles, the facets of a stone hawk,
A carved head with living mouth. She noticed the fleshlike
   curve of the mouth compared
To other lines that met at points and formed hard ridges.
   And opened the book at random. And read that humanity
Was the mould to break from. And, as with each time she
   read this declaration, did not understand.
She saw the young professor who had taught the book,
   standing at his office window,
Seven floors up above the rounded tops of trees, and looking
   out, as she sat by his desk,
As if he had a view of the sea. One shoulder propped against
   the window frame, he described
The swirling yet distinct events of nature, all that he saw
   missing from this place.
He knew a bay where, if this were the ocean, they would see
   pelicans stop in midair
And fall like guided missiles at fish below the surface,
   gulls quarrel over eels
Or crab legs dangling from their beaks. Everywhere the eye
   went—motion, drama. Not this inertia.
He pushed off the window, shrugged. Nothing going on.
   And Iris thought,
"He doesn't know my family." And all that malarky about
   the continent's edge, the stage

Where gods toiled inhumanly, noble gulls climbed shafts
     of sunlight, as if they didn't scavenge garbage.
She'd seen them on the lakes—yes, even this far from the
     sea, here where nothing happened—gobbling fish guts.
But she recognized the story of the drunk whose red horse
     trampled him to death.
She recognized the woman with the child, putting up with
     him, outlasting him.
She hadn't hated Cale, as Jeffers' woman hated her man.
     When Ruth was born,
Cale went sailing. He said it was too much, the c-section,
     the waiting. He didn't see their baby
Till she was two days old. Then, stood at the bed's foot,
     as Iris nursed her, and rocked and rocked,
Hugging himself and rubbing his nose and saying it was
     damn cold in this damn room.
He wouldn't touch the baby, wouldn't touch Iris, and never
     came home from work some nights. One night
Iris had gone to bed after calling and calling his place
     of business (that sign-painter's shop he tried).
She woke past midnight, heard the baby crying and stopped
     herself. "That's not the baby."
She reached for Cale. He wasn't there. "That's some old
     cat outside." But Iris couldn't move.
It wasn't the baby or a cat. To move was to dredge herself
     up from a nightmare depth.
The crying was a growling and a groaning from the baby's
     room. She walked in
And flicked the light on to make the monster vanish in
     the glare, before she faced it.
There he was, curled in Ruth's crib beside her, the baby
     fast asleep in his body's curve.

He was naked and asleep and crying. And Iris said, "Why,
   bless your heart." She'd wanted him right then.
But now, she wanted sleep and read for sleep, the motion
   into sleep—like going west
And rising straight through mountains to descend on a
   sloping plain to something shining
Where the stone dwelling waited with her poet, and each
   animal he loved—hawk, horse, gull,
Sea lion—let him out of his accursed human body and would
   let her in.
Now, she was her poet (this was part of the sleepward dream)
   and she would love what he despised.
And have both worlds—the wild and human, the great and
   petty, a family. But as she crossed
Her hands between her breasts for sleep, left cheek turned
   to take sleep's other blow,
She knew she wanted nothing so grand as sea cliffs or the
   wingstroke of a sea gull.
She wanted touch that would be given and received with
   gratitude, the gift and grace of sanity.

If Iris needed touch, then so did Mama, and she had missed
   it longer, though she had men friends
To drink with at the state line roadhouses, old boys on
   the scout for something a little less ripe.
Then, Mama found Charles. Iris believed luck like Mama's
   had to come from God.
Everybody knew Charles; he was the crossing guard at Kroger's;
   what you'd call a good boy.
Two crosswalks rayed into the parking lot outside the store;
   there, Charles directed traffic.

Stopping the flow when a retired farmer, not looking,
   shuffled across; sometimes,
Pausing to assist an addled old shopper who had lost her
   place. He blocked the traffic
With a gesture or waved cars through, his lips compressed,
   head bowed as if to signal how much
He understood the world's frustrations, the old's especially.
   They stood with laden carts,
Facing the labyrinth and had, sometimes, parents themselves,
   lingering at home. They held up traffic
And couldn't help it. Charles understood. He wore a
   uniform but always held his cap
As if he paid respects to all, his red face friendly, a
   sucker in his mouth,
Like a white thermometer. Even tempered, slow, yet finally,
   capricious. Leaning
Down to hear a crony's story on a hot, slow afternoon, he
   would wave cars through,
And, instead of walking to escort her, signal a woman with
   her cart to cross.
The day that Mama found him he was like that, lackadaisical
   as a nodding thistle.
A bad bearing on her cart made one wheel spin. Mama had
   bought too much and tried to guide
The cart with her beer belly. Charles, ignoring her,
   motioned a car through. There was a wiry, soft
Collision. Mama's cart tipped sideways. Groceries sprayed
   across the asphalt. Charles cursed.
Mama grabbed his forearm like a wader caught by a current
   on shifting stones.
When somebody appeared—the manager?—he whirled on Charles
   and Mama both and shouted.

He grabbed Charles's hat and said he would replace the
   groceries and Charles, too.
So, Charles had needed someone, just like Mama. Truck
   loaded, the poor boy stunned, Mama drove
To the state line and bought them both a beer or two, a
   few games of video poker.
Charles cheered up. You couldn't tell how old he was,
   like those boys on Lawrence Welk
Who dance at show's end with the grandmothers, smiling
   more tenderly than any son.
Unembarrassed, helpful, but a little puzzled, too, to be
   getting drunk like this
With a woman Mama's age. The groceries should not have
   sat out in the truck so long.
Lost a gallon of ice cream, Hoy's favorite kind, and when
   Rice saw it melted on the cab floor,
He screamed bloody murder. But Charles and Mama, happy
   on their high of new love
And beer, appeased him. Gracefully, as when he guided
   traffic on a good and busy day,
Charles cleaned the melted ice cream, head and shoulders
   in the cab, butt wobbling—
Hard work on a warm day—as they watched. Hard not to
   forgive such good will, and they did.

Charles worked the truck patch on the mobile home's south
   side, all spring choosing among the new pale shoots
Which to uproot, and joined Mama in bed, ending her pre-dawn
   muttering, bringing her home
From the state line drunk, unpredictable, but soothable.
   Iris read that earnestness

In going about one's business, earnestness like nature's—
    the rising green stockade of corn,
The heart-shaped bean leaves pairing up and hiding the
    crusted earth—excelled the virtue of art.
Her poet said, "All the arts." At night, Ruth asleep
    beside her Uncle Hoy or Rice,
And they admonished to tuck her in when they turned off
    the TV and went to bed,
And Mama and Charles still drinking at the state line,
    not due till after midnight, Iris took
The second car, a bare-bones Ford Fairlane, unsteady
    on its shocks as the baby in the treetop,
And drove to the university library and there sat late
    with magazines and students
  In the good light that, with night spread against the
    windows, made her reading earnest,
Almost an act of nature. Once, she saw the English teacher
    who have given her
Her poet. She watched him move along the magazine racks,
    taking down
Fat quarterlies and pamphlets and newspapers, and set them
    from A to Z, in a stack, and flip through them,
His shoulders squared like a yoke, the light quivering
    on his glasses. She remembered it,
That look on his face, and knew if she approached him, he
    would keep it for a moment, then—an effort—
Penetrate the coldness with a smile of attention, or at
    least a listening regard.
She spoke to him. She waited for his recognition. But
    saw, even as she reminded him of her poet—their poet—
He was waiting for the interview to end, did not remember
    her, or, if he did,

Did not care. She had taken her seat again and looked at
    the yellowish tableau against the windows,
Her former teacher bent between two stacks of magazines,
    and Iris seated far to his left,
Almost out of the picture, thinking—"I still have Robinson
Jeffers, you sorry son of a bitch."

She still had her ghost husband, Cale, waking her at dawn,
    rapping at the kitchen window,
Hungry for his fix. He thumped his arm and opened his
    beak and begged.
When Iris woke, she saw the titmouse with a sunflower seed
    clamped between claws,
Pecking the black shell, shaking the window glass where
    she had hung the feeder by suction cups.
It was August. Green Indians, eight feet tall, had taken
    over the palisades of corn.
The hedgeapples gave daylight by the house a tint of undersea
    tranquillity.
The female's cloudy womb of leaves bore pulpy, useless fruit.
    When thunderstorms passed over,
Making the two trees claw the roof, the apples, big as
    softballs, boomed on the metal, rolled off
And rolled below the house or into ruts and ditches, to turn
    pale yellow, brown, and soften,
Or be pecked apart. She could not look at them without
    thinking of Cale. But then,
The two trees lunging in the wind, producing this strange
    fruit, turned her mind to Ruth . . .
She knew it would be hot. Out in the drainage ditches,
    far from the road, the marijuana

Flowered like the ghost of the Kentucky hemp fields, weeds
     blossoming pure cash.
She could open windows to the brief dew of morning or let
     the house hoard what coolness it kept.
The air conditioner had shut off. She lay and thought of
     it. How Hoy and Rice would lurch
Into the house and bellow with pleasure at its chill. How
     Mama basked before the roaring unit,
Reading her tabloid. How Iris and Ruth, as if snowbound,
     thought up games. Charles was handy,
If it was broken. The titmouse hammered the seed, the
     hedgeapples offered their tremendous shade.
Coffee time. She sat up, sinking in the breathless pillow
     of the couch, and waited.
She felt along each thigh—thin—and pulled herself out of
     the soft pit with a grunt.
She found her slippers, reached for robe. Cereal for Ruth,
     a bowl that would swell to mush
Under her neglect. Toast later for them both. Eggs and
     ham for Hoy and Rice.
No worry about Charles and Mama. For them, hair of the dog,
     cold beer in the ice box.
They'd be up for lunch. The coffee dripped, accumulating,
     black. She knocked butts
From the TV ashtray on its stand, focus of the ashy sour
     smell of morning in the house,
Until the coffee covered with its fragrance. This was home
     despite all. The pot hushed,
Signaled with a puff of steam, a few last drips. The first
     best cup was hers.
Ruth, half asleep, would stumble to the table. She set
     the cereal there and turned

To watch her birds. Low on seed. A titmouse, finding
　　nothing, looked her in the eye.
Beyond this smooth, reflective plane that showed it only
　　another titmouse, it could detect
Another world with answers for this deprivation. This was
　　not the nature her poet
Loved—unless it was the broken-winged hawk's request for
　　death that he recorded.
Sometimes she thought her thoughts could take her out of
　　the world and she'd be happy. That was transcendence,
Wasn't it? Her teacher might have told her what it was.
　　The wild window-eye
Showed her the ferocity of hunger, and, once again, Cale's
　　face flared in hers.
She heard her brothers waking, stretching, yawning. Ruth,
　　who always woke up giggling, snorted
At a dream joke, and let her eyes open like coin slits,
　　humorless with sleep.
Nothing but snoring from Mama and Charles, both in the
　　master suite. They would wake dry-mouthed,
Half-brained, dazed as mocking birds who fly at their own
　　reflections in plate glass,
Worthless until that first beer, then hardly worth much
　　after that. All her stolen time
Was time that no one knew she stole. Iris held her coffee
　　to her lips. The family stirred.
She thought of her poet's house, built of ocean boulders,
　　on the tongue of lava and granite
By a river mouth to the Pacific. Gulls danced there, as
　　he said they did. The moon,
Waning and wild by day, matched their whiteness. Something—
　　a tree called the dark-leaved Australian—

And the cypress gave shade. Unimaginable, except as the
    fantastic or childlike shapes a word breeds
As images. This place, her home, was full within her, too.
    Rising on the thrill
Of morning coffee, her mind laid down the mottled snakeskin
    of the road through fields, the hot
Smell of pines, the rise where on its clay-pale crest their
    place was mounted on cinder blocks,
Silvery and dew-bearded. The towering corn behind it. The
    double hedgeapples like a wave
Held to shield and not assault, brushing the aluminum roof.
    Look for these, she would say,
Like her poet, when we've hooked the house to a semi and
    the septic tank's caved in and the power lines are down
And the fields gone back to hemp. Look for the glossy green
    throwers of shadow and pulpy meteors.
On this spot a woman harrowed by failure found refuge enough
    with her kin.
Her ghost fills a vial of air for birds, still breeding, riding
    the limber tips of the hedgeapple trees.

Hoy was the fat version of Rice and Rice the skinny one
    of Hoy. Both reeked of Marlboros.
They wore sportshirts with pockets for their packs. They
    loved each other and did small favors
Constantly, like loaning cigarettes, sharing beer. They
    slept in single beds
In one room, bachelors too young yet to seem spinsterish.
    They had separate lives.
Hoy's was a life of endomorphic pleasures; his stations
    of the cross were fried pie at the courthouse cafe,

Ice cream at the DQ, and various forms of fish, flesh, and
    fowl at fast food restaurants.
Rice liked business; slim and smart, he made deals, for
    the new truck, the rented land and trailer, the marijuana crop.
They'd sit below a red oak, sweating, drinking cans of Slice.
    "Gimme one of them,"
Hoy'd say and nod at his brother's pocket. "Now, gimme a
    light." Rice would and drawl,
"You want me to kick you in the chest and get you started,
    too?" Those boys. Iris and Ruth
Would sit with them at lunchtime. Iris egged them on to
    hear them talk. "Which of you remembers
Daddy best?" she'd ask. "Well, I'm a minute older," Rice
    would claim. "So, I believe
I hold the man in mind a minute more than brother here.
    He was a slim old man."
Hoy grinned and said as meanly as he could, "I'd call him
    heavyset." Rice had a way
Of shrugging, like a Frenchman, that implied, "Believe what
    you have never seen, my friend.
But my eyes know." Iris knew that they were lucky; older
    than she, still confident.
They thought a pit bull trained to guard the marijuana plants
    might draw some interest.
They kept, instead, the little dachsund, Crank. He was their
    good luck charm, their pet and mascot.
And he was lucky, substandard and a roamer, returning
    after a month abroad with a bruise
Black as a telephone on his pink belly, his wiry golden
    fur all over burrs,
Ticks swollen in his ears. Given up for lost and then come
    back. Or when he ate

A meal of tossed out chicken bones from the garbage, his
    stomach turned to cast iron, cobbled with points and nubs,
The skin, to the touch, like the surface of a knurled
    ladder step. Yet every bone passed—
A softened, bloody stick. A sweet dog weakening its long spine,
    sitting up to beg,
Hopping steps into the truck. His trick was burying cigarette
    butts. The brothers flicked them
Under the red oak where they sat at lunchtime. Crank's long
    claws found the softer mulch.
Now, they sat, Iris and Ruth on the cloth spread under
    the red oak, the shade warm,
The sunshine hot. Hoy and Rice in the corn, weeding their
    secret crop. Charles and Mama
Had taken the truck to town to buy baling wire. But they
    would come back drunk, with or without.
Ruth followed Crank along the row of red oaks, like columns,
    the windbreak that,
One winter, Iris had seen housing two dozen red tails on the
    leeward side. Walking,
She'd stopped, struck, to see a string of lampshades, the
    hawks' white bellies, along the oaks,
Facing the hacked and empty square of acreage. A day almost
    too cold to walk in,
Except if you were 19, an expectant mother pressed to make
    a big decision.
And she had decided. Two dozen red tails. Her poet never
    saw so many hawks at once.
Ruth called her mother, "Mama, there's two doggies here.
    They're drunk like Charles and Grandma!"
"Drunk doggies, Ruth?" Then, Crank ran out in a circle,
    belly low. Ruth pointed

And stood aside as two fox pups, not much bigger than
    gray squirrels, staggered near her,
Butted a tree with pointed snouts. Crank made a sound of
    pain and Ruth called to him,
"Look, Cranky, doggies! But they're drunk." Iris saw
    the fresh foam on their lips, and one,
Lunging into the other, bit its flank. Both foxes had fresh and
    crusted wounds. One lurched
Against the red oak, bit the bark. Iris grabbed Ruth up.
    Crank dashed between
The foxes, swirling and snapping. Iris called for Hoy
    and Rice. Fat, puffing Hoy ran out,
His hoe a funny, useless looking weapon in his fists.
    "Oh, Crank's been bit by these foxes,"
Iris said, clutching Ruth, as the dogs fought and snarled.
    Dizzy with their rabies,
The foxes bumped together and slipped into the corn. Crank
    barked and chased after them,
Bitten on both ears and on the haunch. "Don't go in there,"
    Hoy shouted, following, flailing
With his hoe blade. He found the foxes and destroyed them.
    Out sauntered Crank, wounded, proud,
And—Iris saw it—doomed. Rice, farther off than Hoy,
    walked out with his three-pronged weeder.
"Some mad foxes have bit our dog," Hoy told him. "Hasn't
    he got his shots, then?" Rice replied.
"Iris?" There was Crank, the bleeding survivor, roamer,
    lucky charm, without a history.
"You tell me, brothers. I have no idea." She held Ruth
    tight who leaned to touch her dog.
They all stood off and flinched as Crank ran up to one,
    then the other, hardly hurt, perky,

A loaded gun. "Well, we could wait and see," said Hoy.
    They looked at Iris, at the child.
Iris gave Ruth a tighter squeeze. Rice said, "Crank,
    come here, boy." The dog limped after him,
Into the towering corn, to the far side of the field, out
    of earshot almost.

That night, dinner over, Charles and Mama not back, Hoy
    and Rice and Ruth, like numb surviving family
Before the television, Iris told herself she'd take the
    old Ford into town.
She would sit in the sad and mellow library light, beside
    the magazine stacks, opposite the windows,
And think of the sentimental poem her poet wrote about
    his English bulldog, buried
Outside the living room window. Sit and wait to see her
    old professor, still a self-absorbed
Young man, cross the plane of night-reflective glass, and
    come to her and whisper an apology.
She knew she shouldn't do it, but, seeing her asleep,
    she scooped up Ruth and carried her back
To Mama's room. She asked her brothers to put her on the
    couch before they went to bed.
Or soon as they heard Mama coming home. Their eddies of
    TV-colored smoke
Circled them. Each clutched a beer and nodded goodbye.
    They'd take care of Ruth. The child woke, demanding
A stack of books to look at. Soon, Iris knew, she would
    slide down the propped up pillow,
The open books piled up like leaves on the babe in the
    woods, the harsh overhead light, making

The room a plain box, without charm, shadowless, except for the
    forest of stuff on Mama's bureau.
"Be sure you move her soon as you hear Mama," Iris said,
    knowing if Mama came home
Drunk she'd want her bed and might wake the child roughly
    and lug her to the couch. Sober,
Mama and Charles would sit with her boys around the TV
    hearth, smoke a few more, have a cold one.
Iris looked back at Ruth propped up in Mama's bed, reading
    her picture books aloud.
She could recite the simple captions as she turned the
    pages, pushing her hair back.
"It needs a trim," thought Iris to herself. She turned
    to Hoy and Rice in the dim room,
Watching the wide, complacent screen change colors, the
    characters pause, washed with canned laughter.
Neither of them laughed. They said, "Good night, Iris."
    And Hoy, "We'll watch the little one."
When Iris opened the door Mama had the handle and swung
    back, rocked on her heels,
And threw her arm back to Charles, slugging him with her
    big pocket book. Iris caught
The hand that let the door go and, with Charles, she held
    her mother steady. Charles's career
Of guiding old, unsteady ladies among cars helped him keep
    his balance, the liquor
Luminous in his friendly face. But Mama's drinking went
    to the base of her brain and stewed there,
Snapping like a live wire loose in a rain puddle. It
    rattled and threw her off.
"Goddamn you going out this door!" she said and pulled
    herself with Iris's help up.

She stumbled in and did a clumsy, pivoting dance of nerves,
  catching a glimpse
Of Ruth down the hall in her own bed. "I ain't got a bed
  tonight, I see.
No, I'm the one's got to shack up on the davenport. Whyn't
  that Cale come and take you both home?"
She opened the refrigerator, grabbed a beer, and popped it.
  A jet of froth flicked
Across her face and in one eye. She squinted. "No, you're
  going to the library."
Charles had taken a seat with Hoy and Rice and laughed at
  something on the TV. They looked
Solemnly at him. "Mama, I have not got time to bicker,"
  Iris said. "I told
The boys to move her when you came home. Now, I'll do it."
  The rocking, bitter woman looked
At the linoleum, beer like a baby on her hip. She asked
  for a cigarette.
Her sons, encircled by the flattening rings of their own
  smoke, did not move. Charles rummaged
The pack from his shirt. The yellow kitchen light stood
  around the drunk woman, the box
Of the TV's haze around the men, the glare around the
  mother and her child.
"I'm putting Ruth in your bed, Hoy, OK?" said Iris. "You
  bet," Hoy answered, glancing,
A sly son, at his mama. "I'm putting you in Uncle Hoy's
  bed until you fall asleep,"
Iris told her daughter. "I'll kiss you when I come home."
  Ruth rode her mother's hip, a book
Under her arm, thumb in mouth, half asleep already. The
  angry yellow woman

Said, "I'm going to bed, then." Her manfriend heard and
    followed, telling everyone a courteous good night.

Iris tried to imagine the life her poet would write for
    her, but the one place he described—
Bare hills, meager grasses, rock like pointed fire that
    she could hardly picture, sea
Underscoring it all with mud-gray body and snarling teeth—
    that place was too noble.
She withdrew from there and reentered the corn and soybean
    squares, the windbreak oaks,
A few upsloping features of terrain, downsloping into
    hollows where creeks cut
Under tree roots. She'd have to make this landscape do,
    even passing through it now
In darkness as she drove. She'd have to make her own life
    immanent in the mind she imagined
For him. All this could be deliberate and instantaneous.
    She would show him that.
If he could choose his death bed by a window, showing
    him the ocean, see the thing
Each day, then, she could make a legend of her life. She
    pounded the steering wheel and wept,
Held tight and slowed to take the curve of bottomland—
    headlights flooding across a field
Of purplish, fleshy, drumstick heads of milo. Beyond,
    an opaque boundary of trees.
What she saw was not herself, a stark figure with a mask
    for face,
Like one of his women. What she saw were small brown frogs,
    like pebbles come to life, in a creek bed.

Above her shoulder, exposed tree roots and the charcoal
    band of topsoil; beside her, Ruth stooping
To pee and holding in each fist a creek frog; ahead,
    Rice and Hoy sloshing in old shoes
Through the quick shallows, snapping fishing lines
    into channels. Now she remembered.
It was an earlier memory of summer, and when she rounded
    the next bend, stopping to catch
A frog for Ruth, who saw them everywhere and couldn't
    make up her mind—a thousand pets!—
Iris knew she would find Charles and Mama underneath a
    laden persimmon tree,
Weighing a branch of fruit in their hands, Mama saying,
    "They won't be sweet for months."
An idyll; an idle thought; an ideal. She shook herself
    to see the event for real. Daydreaming.
But that had been a day and not a dream, and then she
    saw Rice point at small footprints
Beside a pothole in the creek. Ruthie watched his finger
    indicate the patterns
Of mink, racoon, deer, fox, and—Look, he'd said—coyote
    coming back. Clean prints in mud,
From, Rice said, the previous night when they'd come down
    to drink. Iris saw town lights up ahead.
The emptiness around them gave them too much significance.
    She passed the courthouse.
The spotlights on its painted clockfaces showed hands always
    at noon. The border state
Confederate memorial faced northeast. Foam of detergent
    in the bank fountain—
College pranksters. The university parking lot, the
    horizontals of the new library,

The bars of light there. She parked the car. And felt,
    with her coming to a stop, the stillness of the heat
Push close again. It wasn't that her life could not be
    lived here. It was being lived here.
And she was living it. This was her life. But she couldn't
    believe her poet understood it.

That woman you have heard of who returned with her girlchild,
    to the family mobile home,
Parked on a hump of clay beside a forty-acre square,
    entering the daily rhythm
Of that near fatal family—I have been watching her.
    She knows the drunken mother
Is harmless, yet has so declined into her love affair—
    the red-faced boy whose hands
Still smooth with youth pass over her lined features
    in the dark—the daughter must be careful.
The brothers play a dangerous game, yet she winks at it,
    takes the child out to the illegal crop.
Already, losing the little dog should be an omen. The
    crop, cut and hung to dry
In the old tobacco shed, hidden behind persimmons near
    the creek, waits for its buyer.
My eyes are all I have. Lidless, tearless, less expressive
    than a stroke victim's,
They are two dry unflinching points of observation. They
    see her now, in the library.
All along the lit oblong of glass the hard-shelled and
    dusty summer insects
Collide and flail themselves to death. There are boundaries
    we cannot cross. She reads.

Her stillness as she reads, turning the magazine's pages
     with a clockhand's slowness, is meant
As a reproach. So, there is no drama in my life, the action
     says. Then, I'll be still.
Long suffering will start to crease her face in ten years,
     working its way out from the eyes.
Instead of waxing fat, the buffer aging bodies need for
     life, her body will wane,
Frost-hard as a January moon. Predictions. Omens.
     Prophecies.
All to pass the time. She reads. The drama's there inside
     the head of uncurled hair. Or there,
Inside the mobile home, where her brothers doze before the
     television. The daughter
Sleeps, thumb in mouth, among her books. The grandmother
     pillows an aging boy's head
On her breasts. You cannot put off living until ready.
     Life is always urgent, here
And now. It fires at you point blank. And here's a young
     man stopping near her seat. Are they
The only people here tonight? That's loneliness—a library
     on a summer night.
He takes a seat beside her. She puts down her magazine.
     Now they are in profile.
What do I read in this tableau? Solemnity, then laughter.
     Then, agreement. Now,
Out of the glass doors they both come, not yet making
     deliberate contact, but close despite the heat.
The scintillant eruption of their voices, new to each
     other's happiness. Shrill crickets climaxing.
And my eyes rushing back among the stars.

Iris and her professor—Tom—found the August night
   too hot to walk in long,
Like a green pond out in someone's yard that turns
   lukewarm in summer, no more refreshing
Than drinking sea water to quench thirst. He lived
   above a grocery store, among
Smells of its lunch counter, barbecuing, smoked ham—
   quiet after nine but fragrant still.
He flipped the air conditioner on, the sea roar of the
   summer, and they took seats
At his dinner table, white and heavy as porcelain with
   coats of white enamel.
Iris thought, "Life's too short," and looked him in the
   eyes. "Why did you talk to me like that?"
He knew, but answered, "When? Like what?" And she
   surprised herself, saying, "I've got no time for this.
We're here. You came and talked to me so nicely in
   there tonight. Why didn't you before?"
The professor, her professor, was a boy then, confused,
   with a man's way of evasion.
"I'm sorry if I hurt your feelings," though he remembered
   only his own feelings. "Have a beer?"
She looked around the room, low shelves of paperbacks,
   doortop desk, kitchen door, bathroom door.
So little in so small a town. Why so little? She reached
   into her purse. "Ah, yes,"
He said, toasting the book of poetry. "You still read
   Jeffers. Good for you."
She placed it on the table like a gun, a card, an invitation.
   He had to see
The pages swollen from constant reading, the way reading
   had worn the cover corners round.

She saw it in a moment's hesitation, before he drank.
    She, too, took a sip.
His eyes remained on the book cover's creases, white lines
    of force; the poet's charcoaled face,
Facing her, though the carved eyes looked at nothing he
    could see. She might have willed him
To speak, but when he did it was without the previous
    flippancy. "Don't you think it's odd,"
Tom said, "that California in 'Roan Stallion' has
    stayed with Johnny? His presence
Is a punishment for her. Even when the stallion tramples
    him to death,
Killing the horse for her is a greater loss than killing
    the man or letting the horse kill him."
Iris looked at the man across from her, wondering, "Was
    this a test? Was there
An answer that he wanted?" She began to ask, "What do you
    want?" But he leaned forward,
Forearms crossed on the table at his chest, the look on
    his face ("Why, he's no more than four years older.")
Said, "I have always wanted to know this. I think you
    know. Please, tell me if you do."
"I think it's simple," Iris said. "They are married;
    they have a child; they loved each other once.
Without him, what would California do? But that's not
    Jeffers' point. The unhappy story
Of an abusive drunk, his wife and child, is not his point.
    It's what such men could do
To California." Iris sounded so peculiar to herself.
    "Where," she asked inside,
"Did you get all that talk?" But it felt good, this new
    voice talking. And the young professor

Lit up. "Why, it is simple!" he said. "Of course, the
  name's symbolic; the child's, too—Christine,
For the vision of the baby Jesus the mother has. Mother,
  child, and God—the horse."
Tom took a long drink, happy as a scholar in his carrel.
  But Iris wasn't sure.
"That's the problem," she said. "It's always the problem
  with Jeffers. Just when people in his poems
Begin to look like people you might meet some day, they
  go back to being only symbols."
She opened up the book. "Look how she drinks with him,
  the husband. That's what a drunk's wife
Has to do sometimes; and has sex with him; and wishes
  that the drink would knock him out.
But then she runs outside and lures him to his death."
  "That's not her intention," Tom said.
"It's the drama that the story has to have." Iris held
  one edge of the table.
The muscles of her forearm looked like welts. The other
  arm pivoted on its elbow,
Her hand clipping the book, a finger buried between pages.
  "Let me have the book,"
Tom said. "Now, let me read you something." He gave her the
  author's interruption on page 24,
The speech about evolving from humanity, breaking from it,
  as atoms break.
"I don't believe that," Iris said. "Then, why read Jeffers?"
  Tom replied and opened two more beers.
She put her hand across her mouth and spoke through
  parted fingers. "I don't think I can tell you.
I have to. I love the poetry. I think there's something
  else that he's not telling."

Tom laughed. "He tells us everything and more. He makes
    it pretty clear what he believes."
A sob, a shiver in her chest and throat, surprised her.
    Tom reached for her hand,
The one clamped to the table edge. "There's something
    he's keeping back," said Iris, looking down
Into the cover picture at the eyes that did not look at
    her or anyone.
"There's something." And let her hand be opened up and
    another hand, the male hand, enter it.

Iris passed through the next day thoughtfully, as if a
    period of grief had ended.
She recollected touch, her body brought it back, a warmth
    returning here, then there.
Mama and Ruth watched TV all day. Charles worked among
    his squash plants, lifting leaves.
Iris would find herself entranced and pull reluctantly
    away from staring at
Nothing, but it was saddening, like a loss, as when he
    pulled away. She didn't feel
What made her mother quiet, made Charles come indoors every
    so often just to stand,
Drinking a glass of water, behind grandmother and child,
    and watch TV. Iris was happy.
When Hoy and Rice came home that afternoon, the calm lifted,
    crackling like crisp cash.
They shook the kitchen floor. Mama rose from TV-watching.
    Charles followed them in.
The brothers only spoke to one another, pleased with
    themselves, in no hurry to please others.

"Well, that was different," Hoy said and popped a can of
　　beer and took a swallow. Mama watched.
Rice winked at Charles and laid a fat white envelope on the
　　table. "Go get the toolbox,
Mama, will you, please?" Mama, docile with anticipation,
　　brought it
From underneath the sink, the gray tin box that really was
　　a lunch pail with a combination lock.
Rice then replied to Hoy, "Strange little squirt. And
　　that gal with him. That was a girl?" Hoy laughed.
"I'm like you. I think it was. Tougher than him."
　　They both laughed, raising beers to their lips.
A pane of cloud that cooled the afternoon sun slid
　　past and light again turned sharp,
Catching every detail on the kitchen table—the jagged
　　surfaces of crumbs,
A gummy yellow residue no bigger than a baby's palm.
　　Iris pulled her gaze
Away. She stood with Charles and Mama, still ignored
　　by Rice and Hoy. "Tell you what,"
Said Rice. "I'll bet she runs the show." "You think so?"
　　Hoy looked curious. Rice nodded. "Yes,
That tough gal runs the show." And Hoy laughed. "Whatever."
　　Then, Mama, her own trance broken, took a seat.
"You count the money now in front of me," she said. "I
　　got some things I need to buy."

Now they have money and the woman I have been watching
　　thinks she has love. Now
Comes the spending. There is the older woman in new wig,
　　her young lover outfitted

In a slick suit for lounging with her in bars. The brothers
  have attached points of silver
To collar tips and boot toes. They sit below the hedge-
  apples with beers and let the women spend.
Soon the corn will be cut, the stalks dry, then cut, the
  tobacco topped and hung where they dried
Their fortune, the hidden marijuana. Life is good. A new
  freezer hums under the car port.
The woman with the child drives into town to buy red meat
  and chicken and ice cream
To stock the freezer. Full of happiness, she sees how
  the corn walls in the road, then soybeans
Float along beside her, flat green reservoirs. She passes
  the brick bungalows below
Their TV aerials, the hedges of red oak and stands of
  cottonwood and locust, always at a distance,
The tobacco in ranks like plumed warriors. Life has
  changed a bit with love and money.
She dreams no longer of the husband, the addict with his
  bruises that he made her share.
She enters the black rolling meadow of the supermarket
  parking lot,
Bulged up among new building and a fringe of trees. She
  sees things for the first time—
How every tree is just as black among its folds and niches
  as it is green,
How sunlight hangs on each like drapery, like the moist
  heat itself. She notices
Her daughter, almost five, skipping beside her into the
  store, and buys a cheap set
Of jewelry, green plastic bracelet, earrings, and tears
  the objects out of their container,

Lets the child adorn herself. She fills the cart with
  food, two carts, lets the boy
Help her to the truck. She notices the soft mustache,
  like pencil marks, on his lip.
Thin lips, a jutting chin, boy's face and grown man's
  body. And a meanness. Is it in the eyes?
They study her; they fall on the little girl, a wriggling
  Salome in her adornments.
What is it? Disapproval? All this food? The two carts
  he must guide back to the store?
She looks at her daughter, perched beside her in the
  truck cab, green earrings, green as grass,
Necklace, bubble ring, and plastic watch, set off against
  her skin, a peachy rosiness.
She must drive home now and remember love and money and
  a time of liberty
From worry up ahead. The vehicle retraces its way down
  narrowing roads,
Into the increasing isolation, where luck comes in its
  season, when escape is given up.

He almost can imagine me, thought Iris, pulling up beside
  the trailer's door.
And I can almost make him understand by speaking in his
  voice. She opened Ruth's door,
Then called for help with all these groceries. Hoy and
  Rice had been relaxing in the shade,
Charles and Mama trying on new clothes. The old Ford
  was still here. Iris called
With sacks in both arms and heard her mother in her voice,
  screaming, "Somebody

Get their butt in gear!" Ruth had hopped right up the
    steps, swung open
The door and stepped in. The air conditioner roared and
    dripped, its damp mark of condensation—
A place on the sun side of the house where butterflies
    edged down and put out their tongues.
Iris took hold of the door handle and wedged a hip
    inside and said again, "Will someone . . . ?"
She heard a doglike moan turn human. There they lay,
    the four of them, face down, arms bound
Like chicken wings, in the living area. Ruth stood at
    their feet and said, "That's Uncle Hoy and Uncle Rice.
That's Charles. That's Grandma," as if making sure
    she knew the names.
They all looked scalped at first. Mama's wig, a bloody
    ball, lay just above her head.
She was moaning, cut down to the bone by the shotgun blast,
    but still alive. Alive,
As Ruth and Iris were, thought Iris. Alive as we are,
    the two sacks in her arms. "That's Grandma's wig,"
Said Ruth. Iris saw the woman move. "That's Uncle Hoy
    and Uncle Rice and Charles,"
Said Ruth again. And Iris, in the last moment before
    acting, found herself
Thanking God for Ruth's sake they had gone to Kroger's.

The cops stretched yellow tape around the mobile home.
    Iris and Ruth found shelter with Tom.
Mama recovered in the county hospital. Hoy, Rice, and
    Charles were stored for later.
School was beginning. Iris could tell Tom saw her now as
    one with Ruth. Females in distress.

No talk of poetry. No silences together. Besides giving
    sympathy,
All he said was "Freshmen to advise. Lots of work." But
    did his breakfast dishes
And Ruth's and Iris's before leaving for the day. Then,
    it was to the hospital
To sit with Mama. Or to the police station to answer
    questions. It was simple
To say, "Yes, it could have been drug-related." Mama would
    know, but Mama couldn't talk.
The money in the toolbox, under the sink (which had not
    been touched), that was their money.
They had no bank accounts. The police looked at her and
    understood. The FBI
Appealed to her intelligence. They complimented Ruth's
    beauty and appealed
To Iris as a mother. They did not know about her poet who,
    in her ear,
Was saying that the quiet places called for quiet suffering.
    And she retorted.
No one could hear but when her eyes would harden an
    interrogator paused and leaned
Toward her as if to listen. She retorted inwardly, "I don't
    think it was quiet.
It wasn't on a cliff above the ocean, among cypresses and
    boulders.
It wasn't quiet. Goddamn your presumption." Still, as
    questions tapped at her and dislodged
Nothing, her poet was all she had to talk to. Mama in her
    hospital bed slowly
Came back, her poor head fringed with ragged hair, the blast
    having mowed the skull dome clean.

But she was empty, bare, as soon the hedgeapples would
     be. Iris bought her a new wig,
But she preferred a red bandana, as if to keep her bloody
     scalp in memory
Of her two sons and her young manfriend. Burying them
     took half of what they had. Iris counted
The months ahead, the money in the toolbox. The police
     untaped the trailer.
The last cloud of FBI dust, driving out to the field's
     far edge for evidence,
Faded. Iris brought Ruth and Mama home. The cut corn
     was that dishwater stubble
That Iris hated, the blunted growth of nightmares. She
     saw knots of winter wheat
In other fields and their own field with its stalks uncut,
     just waiting, like wicker to be woven,
Like, she thought with dread, a field of matchsticks.

Her poet apologized for bad dreams. There was still in
     the living room rug, when they returned,
The purple brown remains of the shooting. Mama went
     directly to the TV
And Ruth, pausing a moment to survey and remember, joined
     her grandma. Iris rolled the rug up,
And found the peppered shot holes in the plywood flooring.
     They looked, in their maroon wash,
Like holes in roses. At this, she wept. When Ruth stood
     by to comfort her, she wanted to say
That she was sorry, too, for her bad dreams. But, unlike
     her poet's, these were real.
In her dreams, she was alone, watching the money dwindle
     in the toolbox, her lover vanish

Into his reluctance—Was it fear?—and two children, Ruth
and Mama, to look after.
Mama held something back. She could take care of herself.
It was as if, like Tom,
She had decided to be an absence in Iris's life that Iris
had to care for.
And Iris couldn't tell the absences from presences anymore.
Was someone out there?
If not close, now, still hidden by the dark that hung beyond
the circle of porch light?
And if not on that close perimeter, then watching up the
road? And if not there,
Then headed back this way with loaded shotguns? And if
not, then sitting together, a knot
Of killers plotting to come? She saw Cale with them, and
Tom, whispering about the dry corn,
The toolbox with a thousand dollars left, and all that
bird seed, Cale said through split beak.
And Tom, showing his ruffled breast of sheet-white down,
flapped his wings and said, "Except
The penalties, I'd sooner kill a woman than a hawk!" Iris
woke. Grinning
At the TV, Mama watched a black and white old movie.
Inside a house, a man and woman
Went berserk with fear, running from window to window.
Outside, figures lurched into
The light, out of a curtain of shadow that combed back
from their bodies, until, lit head to toe,
Off kilter, they came to hammer on the walls and windows.
Ruth had found her way to bed
In Uncle Hoy's bed. Iris flicked off the set and Mama
whined. She changed the channel

And Mama was content with Johnny Carson. He was talking
    about the weather
In Los Angeles. Iris stuck her head outside. There was
    the first frost-bitten moon
Of December. She could hear a drop of moisture on a fallen
    leaf freeze with a ping.
And then the uncut corn began to talk—a windless whispering
    of dew becoming ice.
Both gas tanks of the truck were full. She heard her poet's
    voice say, "California," as if
He called a woman's name. And the brittle comedian on
    the TV chattered in agreement.

II

Iris found her mother and child another life, driving
   sixty hours
Across the continent. To keep awake she built it stone
   by stone, as she had read
Her poet built his life. She drove the new truck with
   its double gas tank south, southwest,
And west. And where she'd find the blocks to build did
   not concern her. Through Arkansas away from snow,
Between the white waste of stars and the desert horizontals,
   among levels of ash
And indigo rising at dawn in Texas. At twilight in New
   Mexico, through basins like blankets
Stitched with fire, unrolling. Iris measured pure imagination
   with discipline,
Building the road ahead as Ruth lay on Mama's lap and Mama
   stared or whimpered,
Like a dog dreaming of chase, and stirred her limbs. Iris
   built the road and watched it curve
Out a white peninsula in azure water. She built a house
   of stones that weighed no more
Than loaves of bread, each dense with sustenance. She set
   the windows firmly, eyes of glass
That mapped the day and turned inward in lamplight. She
   put her mother on the front porch
To gaze out at the ocean, Ruth in the front garden playing,
   and herself to scan
Her fragment of creation—setting gulls to rock on newmade
   waves, white caps farther out,
The sun to turn on and off with floats of passing cloud.
   There was a moment when she saw only
Herself in this imagined world and left the body at the
   wheel, her passengers

Sleeping in care of a ghost. Iris saw herself in a new
   body, pivoting
In midair, her wingspan like an overarching thought.
   Below her in the water, she sighted
A hovering, unwary, tear-shaped, silver motion, and fell
   at it, parting her bill
Amid the gray explosion of the contact, snatching the quarry,
   twisting to the surface,
Juggling the fish around headfirst to let it enter, smooth-
   slick, down the open gullet.
Iris woke. She urged the truck's bulk back between the
   night-bright lines. To plan or dream, to keep
Awake for all of them, she took the thermos full of quick-
   stop coffee between her thighs,
Unscrewed the cap, poured liquid in the cup balanced on
   one thigh, screwed cap back on, and drank.
A semi blasted past, a crashing through of lighted immanence,
   blaring its warning.

Down through the Angeles Forest they descended, passing
   through fire patches, downshifting loops
Of creeping traffic, each car sealed against the milky
   smoke that rippled over grasses,
Turned coal-colored by fire. The trees themselves stood
   back off these bare slopes, twice-shy, but watching.
Mama, her head wrapped in the red scarf, dozed against
   the window. Ruth, awake, sat forward,
Hands on the dashboard, watching fire unfurl its banners
   past them like a big parade.
Iris, too tired to reproach her, aimed at the car in front,
   guiding the truck in low gear,

Aching it into third when traffic eased and rolled on
    faster and the bigger truck
Behind her filled the side mirror. She worked her tongue
    around her mouth, gums acidic with fatigue.
For all her exhaustion's bitterness and burning, she
    wanted most to stop and brush her teeth.

"I need to find the water," Iris told the station attendant
    in Ontario.
He sworded in the dipstick and raised his head like a
    farmer from his hoe and gazed into
The distance northwest toward Los Angeles. The landscape
    rose and met a solid plane
Of smog, as brown as dry earth, promising heat. "I never
    been to the beach," he said. "Lived here
All my life. Funny. I'll get you a map." Ruth drank
    a Coca Cola. Mama's
Frozen gaze was perfect, saying, "Nothing changes; you
    can change skies." (But what was this
Stinging curtain hanging down like an unravelled dirty
    bandage?) "You can't change minds."
Another voice, banal and unprophetic, spoke to Iris,
    "What beach you headed for?"
As if among all possibilities, its owner could point out
    a place's charms.
Iris noticed she was looking down at him, and wished she
    had her Mama's help.
He looked like someone. Who? Impeccable, his moustache
    jaunty as a dragonfly, his chest,
A butterfly of muscle pressed against his shirt, the
    biceps tight in the short sleeves—

Clark Gable? Mama stared, a mannikin, through the wind-
   shield. Ruth gulped her Coke and soon
Would say she's hungry. "I know the beach," he said.
   "You folks from Kentucky, are you? Vacationing?"
Black hair with Vitalis combed into it, brown eyes, skin
   tanned like Hoy's and Rice's by work
(Though it was pleasure, she would learn). He took the map
   from the attendant and spread it
On his car hood. The car, a Buick, looked like a piece
   of sky in spring, its chrome trim
Like places where thin clouds reflected glare. He traced
   a route across the map's midsection,
That ended at the blue expanse of ocean. "I live here,"
   he said. "In fact." And tapped a word
That jutted like a pier into the water. Iris had hoisted
   Ruth to her hip
And listened. Then caught the image of herself as country
   wife, learning
The land surveyor's plans to flood her farm. She shook
   it from her head. He caught the nuance,
Looked at the lady in the truck, the child—too big to
   be picked up—on Iris's hip,
At Iris herself, taller by a forehead, a skinny woman
   aged by leanness, long-faced, drawn,
Her ponytail pulled back through a thick rubberband.
   Practical, not girlish. She looked down at him.
There was a hollow at her throat where collarbones began,
   her sharp hips flared,
And something in her eyes—an average gray—something looked
   out with a hawk's intensity.
He didn't know just what to say. He asked again, "You're
   on vacation?" Stating it as if

He half-wished it were true. He gave Iris his card—E. Smith,
    Beachcomber Salvage—
And let her follow him. He led them on the elevated river
    of the freeway,
Over miles of suburban plains, houses as dense as fields
    in August. Though December,
They drove with windows open, the sky's gray holding in
    a muggy warmth. Mama let her face
Be bathed by it. Smith did not mean to lose them, but at
    a small rise off the freeway, he honked
And pointed out at something pushing in, below a band
    of coffee-colored haze.
Iris braked to peer at it—the ocean. But when she looked
    back she had lost her guide.
"I've lost him now!" she wailed and Ruth, afraid to see
    her crying, cried, too, in encouragement.
And Mama, her stare budged like a heavy stone, added a
    a dull moan. Iris pulled over and hugged
The steering wheel, its empty, round embrace. "I've lost
    him now!" He leaned in at her window.
"You haven't lost me. You're going to be all right." A
    neighborhood of pastel-colored houses,
Like toy blocks, stood around them. Up ahead, a busy
    intersection, and beyond,
Another group of houses, then the ocean. "Now," Smith
    told her, "you're coming home with me.
You haven't lost me. But one thing is for sure. You
    folks aren't on vacation. I can see that."

That night the weather changed in a new way, as if the
    air were fanning mist that Iris

Couldn't see. Not too cold, but Iris felt the change.
    She came indoors
With sleeping bags from the truck, and set them down, and
    looked out the front window at the street.
Mama was propped in front of the TV, and Ruth asleep in
    E. Smith's bed. Iris watched
It coming, what she'd felt condensing from the air. The
    street lamps lost their blazing edge
And turned as soft as fireflies. The lit air was like
    feathers. Fog, of course. But not the stuff
That stood in half-stripped hollows on fall mornings in
    Kentucky—that freshwater creature.
She watched this thing half-walk, half-hover down the
    street outside, a massive dissolution,
Trying to put itself together around the street lamps and
    put the lights out, too. From salt water,
Deep water. She unrolled the sleeping bags for Mama,
    Ruth, herself. Smith lingered, said, "Fog's thick,"
And brought Ruth to the couch. He was a bedtime reader
    and light angled from his room. It spread
A faint fringe of illumination out into the livingroom.
    Iris opened
The torn and taped paperback of poems. Time to buy a new
    one. She had reached the state
Her poet wrote about, but didn't think of it like that.
    Rather, she saw herself,
Her mother, and her child in safety. They had made it
    to a safe place, where, before sleep,
Iris read about the elements of nature, about Pacific
    fog appearing suddenly,
A mystery, Jeffers called it, and how fishing boats moved
    cautiously along the shore—

Earnestly—to keep themselves intact, steady as the aim
    of pelicans or planets.

The morning rang a yellow gong outside the windows. Wind
    vibrated the glass panes.
The house was hot. Its heat reflected on Ruth's brow.
    Mama licked sweat off her upper lip.
Wind pressed the windows and released. Iris had gone to
    sleep in her travel clothes. She itched.
She rose and found Smith in the kitchen stirring a sunny
    bowl of eggs, squinting outside,
Frowning. "Santana winds," he said. "Began last night.
    Only time you need A/C."
He looked sidelong as if afraid to see her in a nightgown
    or just to see her there.
He whisked the eggs. "You'll have to like them scrambled,"
    he said. "Sorry about the heat.
I'll open the house, though it won't help much. Only
    the water helps." Iris frowned.
"At the beach," he said. "Being in the water." He set
    the pan down, gas jets sprouting on the stove.
Their hiss made Iris open her eyes wide and Smith adjusted
    the loose, orange flame
To a tight crown of blue, and set the butter wandering
    in the skillet. House heat swallowed
The stove's heat. Wind leaned again against the kitchen
    window and let go, shaking the glass.
The sun rained down in smog blown, Smith told her, from
    the inner basin. Dressed like the day before,
His back curved round and stout, Smith was an oak stump
    in a floral shirt, in shorts and sandals,

His hair combed into one slick-piece, like patent leather.
   Reaching her arm to him,
Iris felt his shoulder at a level below hers and grasped
   it, then the other.
He paused, crouching like a startled cat, then turned
   the gas off, carefully.
She knew her clothes stuck to her like wet paper. Her
   skin itched. She should ask to take a shower.
She saw his nipples through the cotton cloth, when he turned
   around. Her body as awake,
But weary, offering nothing but a hungry gratitude. They
   pressed together,
Her night sweat dampening his chest, his arms. Then,
   Mama flicked the TV on and Ruth
Giggled, the laugh she woke up with, and Iris said,
   "I have to get a shower."

That afternoon Smith took her to his warehouse. He pulled
   his sky-blue Buick
Into a space beside a chain link fence in an alley of gray
   gravel and white dust.
Key in the padlocked gate, he swung it open for her along
   a groove the frame had dug.
"I met her at the beach." He had to tell her why he'd
   come out to Ontario.
"She had something, you know?" Ranked on the right but
   out of place in the open sunshine,
Refrigerators, all the older models, one or two with turban
   generators.
Then, on the left, oddments of lumber, panels and boards
   of varnished flaking wood, a group

Of rusting engine blocks. "Her name was Cathy. She wasn't
    from around here, I could tell.
Pale as . . . as white as that refrigerator there,
    and lying dry-skinned in the sun.
God, I could not believe it." Iris followed through the
    open yard. She saw machinery
She didn't recognize, bulbous-headed things with sharp
    attachments, tables sprinkled
With sawdust or steel filings. They went into the shade
    of an open shop, beside the warehouse,
Where empty paint cans, rusted metal poles with ridges
    lay in cool cobwebs.
"So, there I was," Smith said. "A Sunday off from work.
    My radio, my cooler of beer,
Just lying out and oiling myself up. I see her. It's
    hot. She's lying by herself. I say,
'You're gonna burn.' And she says, 'What was that?'
    I say again, 'Miss, you are going to burn.'"
Another key in padlock, sliding open a wooden door on
    rollers to the warehouse dimness,
Like a cave's dark, after the summer glare, the coolness
    palpable, a body of air.
Down a low concrete ramp, past wire cages, storage areas.
    "Well, soon I lent her
My suntan lotion. Then, she had a beer. And then, I got
    her story—part of it.
She's from this town Ontario. I say, 'Canada?'" The
    stink of paint and basements mingled
With something else—tranquillity of things out of the
    weather, come to a resting place,
Like travellers inside a caravanserai. Or one of those
    museums, Iris thought,

Where you can stand before a roped-off livingroom or antique
   barber shop. She saw
A cage of steamer trunks, some with brass fittings. Then,
   boxes of paperbacks, westerns and sci-fi.
Smith let her stand and gaze. He kept on talking,
   "Ontario—it's out where I met you."
Here in an open place a small crane stood, holding aloft
   an engine like a sculpture.
Along the walls were washers, dryers, furniture—a massive
   vanity reflected
The engine in its mirror like a beauty's face. "Losing
   her was hard," Smith said.
"She wouldn't marry me. The whole time we're together,
   it's this cop in Ontario
She's trying to make jealous. Cathy." He shook his head
   and reached into his pocket
And shook his change and keys. "She did burn, too, by
   God. Bright red, for all my Sea and Ski."
They stood now looking down a hall at two faint images
   that, when Smith flicked on a light,
Startled Iris, turning clear and harsh. It was the two
   of them, below a sign
Stating in flat red letters: THIS IS HOW THE CUSTOMER
   SEES YOU. She saw
Her thin self in capris, a blouse, beside a shorter man
   with rounded shoulders.
She would grow thinner and he would grow fatter and even
   now they looked together
Like one and zero. Counting down or up, thought Iris,
   or she might have thought. Smith noticed
Nothing, but switched his office light on on the left.
   The secretary's desk, his desk,

A newly purchased .45 with loaded magazine. He made a
   last remark.
"You know, I even thought of this." And hefted the ugly
   gun, then laid it down atop
A stack of invoices, behind the desk and out of sight.
   "It's time to have a drink."
He led her down the hallway to the mirrored door; a key;
   steps down into a bar.
Door shut, she saw it was a two-way mirror. Inside his
   private bar, Smith watched his men
Check in and out (The time clock was out there and pigeon
   holes for orders). The two-way glass
Tinted the vista green and gray. A mirror above the bar
   was cracked across,
The mar an emerald flaw that showed the inner meat of
   glass, its urge to break and cut.
On walls, crossed swords and bayonets, machetes. In a
   rack, all vintages of rifles.
Stacked on two coffee tables, magazines for men—cars,
   and skin and the outdoors,
All dogeared, bushed with moisture, fingering. Smith
   said it was all salvage. All of it
Nothing that anybody wanted from the fires or floods his
   men cleaned up.
She saw a chess set and a set of dominoes, the white squares
   and pips dimmed by smoke.
Behind the bar the humming fridge looked new but metal
   showed in scars and dents. She chose
A stool with vinyl seat intact. Others grinned stuffing
   or were taped. Below the bar
The glasses were all sorts in neat rows. Smith had passed
   his stage of mournful reminiscence.

He smiled and set two glasses on the counter. "We call
   it 'The Total Loss Room.' What'll you have?"

The eye looks through an emptiness to see. And that gap
   closes against too much light
And opens in the dark so wide it matches the void of
   vision with a void of space.
What we see through is an emptiness. Through hers, Iris
   saw rescuer and rescued
Flowing together. Beyond her, though, it looked like
   an occupation—the little land
Of Smith invaded by an overwhelming number, two homeless
   women and a child.
Her poet always took the larger view, seeing in netted
   fish the death of cities,
Believing poems cleansed humanity, at least somewhat.
   Iris saw herself,
Her daughter growing up, her mother holding steady in
   forgetfulness, and Smith,
Making each day another day of life, where Mama watched
   TV, Ruth went to school,
And Iris, keeping house for him, could keep meals warm
   when he came home late drunk. She read
Her Vintage paperback of Jeffers and felt his voice,
   tugging her north.
The bay's south side was close and curved along a green
   peninsula, but the northern curve
Ended in mountain silhouettes. Thus, distance added to
   the voice—apparent distance—
And made an answer seem impossible. For Iris, looking
   outward always ended

In the short view—the day and the day's end. The longer
    vistas opened up inside her.

And so, she came to live among bare streets, with not a
    tree except the crooked saplings
And squat palms and, in the distance, a line of eucalyptus,
    dark-leaved Australian clouds.
Around Smith's house, that became her house and Ruth's
    and Mama's, there were gardens like candy boxes.
All up and down the street, desert flower and cactus gardens,
    gardens of colored quartz.
Gravel gardens without a single plant! Where only color
    was important,
But color that would last the whole year through. The
    houses, too, all pastel blue and pink
And yellow, sunbleached many of them, were squares of color.
    Their lawns were parched or barnacled
With sprinkler heads that burst on suddenly and kept a
    patch of spongy grass dew-bright
At three p.m. Sometimes she'd glimpse a crone with long-
    necked key, cranking sprinklers on,
Leaning above a mass of dusty ivy, and see herself behind
    the flaring screen
Of years. And there were gulls, swinging above the school-
    yards, parking lots of taco stands
And ice cream parlors, and the ocean that her poet said
    was a stone, sharp-edged, polished
To shining. Floating in a haze of smog and sunshine, still,
    it was the medium
Of seasons. It changed color like the great hedgeapples
    in Kentucky that swept the roof.

A cold, ferocious blue by winter solstice, then into summer,
    turning milky
Sapphire, and always under overcast the color of the
    cloud, or with a change
Of current—pea-green or chick-pea yellow mixed with ash
    and pearl. Maybe these were wrong, maybe
Never in a lifetime would she record the ocean's color
    for a chart of seasons.
Before she ever saw it face to face, it was a solemn,
    grainy black and white.
Along it now, a boulevard of sand ran straight, blond,
    studded with blue lifeguard stations,
Curving north into the line of mountains, south ending
    in the humped peninsula
Of red tiled houses pointing at the ocean. She saw no
    resemblance to her poet's
Landscape. Here people abounded; beaches, strands, and
    piers were made for them. No rocky tidepools,
No granite promontories, tors, or tongues of lava. No
    stage for mad heroics. Just as well.

Look on the woman now as she is looked upon, with wonder,
    by her family,
Beside the bulbous eye of the Pacific, that looks here
    like a piece of inlaid wood,
The arc of the horizon and the jigsaw edge that locks
    into the coastline, wrinkled
At each end of the reach from Point Vicente to Point Dume,
    so shallow in its bite,
So blurred by haze and distance; from her end it goes
    north and vanishes. Look at her wish

To do the same. And she has heard about the canyon just
    offshore, an omen plunging
Over fourteen hundred feet straight down, through mud and
    gravel into grottoes where
Monsters breed—the phosphorescent jellyfish, like eyes
    plucked out, that live and choose
Blindness or pure vision, turning inward, unencumbered
    by light. She cannot look
East, back where she came from. There, behind the wall
    of smog, the mountains rise. The past
She fled from, for her life, her daughter's and mother's
    lives, is there concealed. And yet,
She looks in no direction they can understand. Her
    daughter asks, "Why are you staring?"
The man whose life she entered and took over will bend
    and say, "What's that, baby?"
And touch her shoulder and see nothing. Even her mother,
    in her garden seat, following
The sunlight like a sunflower, will, when Iris peers at
    something no one else can see,
Adjust her own stare slowly to aim where Iris aims. Yet
    no one thinks
To ask, "What are you thinking, Iris?" Always it is,
    "Iris, what are you looking at?"
And she will answer, "Something I just noticed for the
    first time," pointing to a flaw
In fabric, a ripple in window glass, a pigment mark below
    the bleached hairs of her arm—
But always to deflect the thing she sees, the thought
    so many fathoms deep.
Perhaps, because she can look to sea so easily—that it
    is simply there—

That makes her thoughtful. At one time she would dwell
  upon the shadow of the great hedgeapples
Outside the window in Kentucky, the way the leaves in wind
  all pointed like a school
Of clear green fish, the furrowed orange bark, the chicka-
  dees advancing out on twigs
Before the leap to the window feeder. So much distinction
  in so small a space. But here,
The ocean is one plane of thoughtfulness, monotonous at
  first, like earth or dust
Or sand, but looked at closer, various and frighteningly
  subtle. Peered at through
Its glinting changes or in overcast you can sink your
  eye into it, plunging
Through sight and back into the pupil's emptiness. A surfer
  angles down a wave,
A pleasure craft zips past, a freighter changes the horizon
  like a cloud, three men
Lie face down in their blood—Hoy, Rice, and Charles—and
  a child's voice shouts, "Look, Mommy!"
And the sun's glare on metallic water throws the speaker into
  silhouette. Again,
The little girl, her daughter Ruth, asks in simple wonder,
  "What are you looking at?"

Years passed, and still she was not sure, except that it
  was in the words she read, or when
Not reading, in the memory of them. To live life otherwise
  was strange to her.
She read her poet, delved for what he called "the honey
  of peace." Once, waiting in Smith's office,

The afternoon Ruth graduated high school and would walk
    across the stage set up
On the unchalked football field, a handsome girl in robe
    and mortarboard, with only one
Nightmare sunk in childhood's boneyard—the raw scene
    of three men lying face down, heads shot off,
And a grandmother moaning, trying to crawl into her wig
    again—Iris tightened.
She looked at what her life was. She was waiting for her
    husband. (That's what she called him now.)
And he was lingering in his bar, having a quick one with
    some friends, some business partners.
She looked down at the .45, a paperweight, on the stack
    of carbons, invoices,
That curled up at the edges from the weight. Wedged into
    the pile was a greeting card.
She worked it out, not wanting to pick up the L-shaped
    gray thing, mean and efficient-looking.
It was a card from Ruth, some Father's Day, the third year
    or the fourth,
When it was clear that Smith would have to do as father.
    Ruth's first cursive signature,
Like a sprout unbending in a cup of earth, above it just
    as carefully executed—
The word "Love." Iris held the card and looked back
    at the gun. Her pleasure just in staring,
Itself like a retreat into a shell of peace, began to
    cloy and sicken her.
She had been shrewd to understand what he had offered,
    young and still ambitious, commander
Of a fleet of panel trucks, viceroy of a warehouse full
    of salvage. He had inflated

Like King Farouk and wore a shriner's fez—his local
    trademark; his pencil-thin moustache
Became a line of ash across his lip; his features widened
    and grew shallower,
Like an image on an overblown balloon. The business made
    its way among the beachtowns,
More and more resembling what it took on—waveson and
    by-blow, wreckage of fire and flood.
He tried to branch out, marketing deodorizing clocks that
    sprayed a stinking perfume
Of cough syrup at intervals the customer could time. Smith
    liked the smell. She looked
Down at the gun. As a child once, she saw a coil of chain
    beside a railroad track.
It looked so light and useless, like a snake skin, that
    she kicked it, pulling her groin against
The stubborn weight. She thought of how Smith, when he
    did come home, prolonged his entry, first
Pausing to retrieve and read the mail (She watched him
    from the kitchen window), the car
Still running as he read the bills and flyers, then the
    progress up the weed-cracked drive,
Under the pyracanthas, pausing to let a cedar waxwing,
    drunk on the shrub's red berries,
Flutter aside (an act of fellow-feeling), then a lurch,
    the roar
Before he turned the engine off in the garage. What
    made him, she would wonder—
Within a pocket of a larger wonder—what made him gun
    a standing engine and
Slam the car door like an explosive plunger? Then, he'd
    dally in the dim garage.

Did he sit inside the car inside that cave? Out he came,
    to tour the backyard's
Corners and edges, the arbor with its ancient Dr. Pepper
    sign, its spiderwebs,
Checking, he once claimed, for black widows. She'd wrap
    a towel around her fist, unwrap it, dig
Beans out of a can, plop them in a sauce pan, clap the
    lid on, set the gas ablaze,
And pour a pool of oil into a frying pan, heating it till
    it showed the runners
Of dense, gold, heated oil, and lay the first tortilla
    to warp and bend, still waiting for him.
Then, she would hear him fussing with the hose—to water
    what? The half-bald yellow lawn?
The evergreen and always dusty ivy? To douse the cedar
    waxwings in the bushes?
She'd sprinkle chili powder in a pan of gray ground beef,
    stirring the mixture bitterly.
His key would scrape the lock. For pity's sake, the door
    was never locked! And, resolutely,
He would retreat, out to the car again, again the engine
    roar, the swift reversal
Out to the empty street. Long after dinner time he would
    repeat it all again.
Ruth sleeping, Mama out before the TV, Iris herself bending
    to the set—
She'd hear the second coming home, for good this time, as
    drunk or drunker than before.
She stood up, shook these daydreams from her head like
    dandruff, and walked into the hall.
She faced the mirror on the bar door, knowing Smith could
    see her through it. Dressed in gray,

Her pocketbook in hand like a sack of fruit, her broad-
    brimmed hat with paisley band, with its "touch
Of whimsy" (Ruth's request), and shadowed under it the
    face she knew, her own—the jaw
Set to complete a task, defeat an obstacle, to gather up
    her strength and speak.
A woman a man once, when she was young, compared
    to a honey locust, thorns and all—
With pale green pinnate leaves, the shape of some religious
    medals, thin as paper, turning
Gold in fall. A hardwood sheathed in silk. She knew it.
    She didn't want to pause and let him
See her. She knew exactly what she looked like, strode
    quickly to the door, and opened it.

Smith did not understand her inner life and could not tell
    you how she had driven his life
Inside. The hours he spent inside his private bar, the
    way he poured inside himself
A sense of life, the body he had lost himself inside,
    growing its distant surface,
And how along the limits of his apprehension life he was
    also part of, somehow,
Was lived, as if he were a planet, a source of raw material,
    on fire inside,
But helpless, sensing far away along the skin the keen
    exploiters' footsteps.
He did not understand his inner life, but knew he had to
    make up for a lack
Of rain. It never rained and when it did, the alien green
    that followed burned,

Igniting weeds from sandbanks, sidewalk cracks, coaxed
  worms like arteries to bleed across
The mirror-gray of concrete, snails to start up garden
  walls—thin-shelled, green blobs of flesh.
He felt the semi-arid landscape where he lived, the climate
  and its beasts and flowers,
And how when sun returned, cut off from damp, they died.
  The weeds paled, turning yellower
Than match fire, worms curled into blackened shoestrings,
  snails glazed over their moist feet and dropped
From walls to crack like crabs and die, gobbled up by
  ants. The sound of rain
Fell between Smith and the distant world. It was the
  bourbon roar he stoked all day.
The business ran itself. His squad of Mexicans, all
  younger men, and the older ones,
The gnarled and knotted Oklahomans from his navy days,
  went out and brought back salvage.
He had a secretary, an accountant who had a secretary.
  The business ran itself.
The ocean seeped below a beach house, soaked its hard-
  wood floor to soggy cardboard, stained
The claw feet of its antique chairs. His men went out
  in panel trucks. They offered
His drying fans and deodorizing clocks, black cherry
  scent, his favorite.
Each week he lunched with the Kiwanis Club, all of them
  small businessmen and one
Sky pilot—face like a woman's on a box of soap, scrubbed,
  hairless, glistening.
Smith listened to talks about the Russian navy and watched
  slides, while munching pickled herring.

The high school club they sponsored put on ties and joined
  them once a month, and sat wide-eyed,
Watching their antics. The preacher's boy was there, slope-
  shouldered from weight-lifting; his father's smile—
A squeaky clean benevolence—picked him out, a nudge
  said, "Yes, my boy."
Yes, this life ran itself, just like his business, like
  the weather, or a power window
He lowered to let the streaming peace of speed in or
  raised, closed off and tinted, behind the roar
Of bourbon, his inner rain. Life ran itself, was good.
  Why couldn't he go home? After work,
He made his accountant stay, who drank diet colas and
  ate nuts for an hour. Smith sat alone,
Thinking how soon the bourbon would wear off and he
  would need another dose, a splash,
Bracing as aftershave, enough to see him home. Why
  couldn't he go home? To Iris,
Floating from room to room with chores, her mother facing
  the buzzing mirror of TV
Like a mirror, Ruth asleep or doing homework. One day
  three females washed against his shipwreck
And joined their destinies to his. He drank the nut salt
  from the bowl and chewed his ice.
The bourbon drizzled in his ears. Time to go home. Let
  the car run him home, top down,
Along the esplanade, the ocean on one side to keep him
  honest, maybe a moon
To point his turn out, light his driveway, mingle with
  pyracantha leaves, the pear tree
And olive holding blessings out in welcome. He would gun
  the engine gently, see

The one light still on in the kitchen window, pause, sit,
     take the same route back. But when
It rained the richness of the world made him want closure,
     an end to repetition. Rain
Was a UFO, but made him feel an obligation had been met,
     a duty fulfilled,
Like stroking Iris's thin flank (she wanted less of that)
     and buying Mama a TV,
And signing Ruth's report card. They never left. They
     were his family. They ran themselves,
Without his love, like rain, but willing to accept it with
     upturned face, made wet,
Refreshed or drenched right to the scalp (his thinning
     scalp). He sobered far more quickly
Than he wanted. It never rained. And life came crawling
     out of it, the distant life
He knew he had to feel to be alive. So that was why,
     every day, he made it rain.

Waking, the morning of her daughter's wedding, Iris left
     her husband still asleep—
The hump of him white-sheeted like a whale of snow—and
     looked in on her mother. The wedding
Was poised, a roll of ribbon, to unwind perfectly—Ruth's
     survivor's elegance.
There would be lunch and then a farewell gathering and
     Ruth and her young carpenter
Would rise in their hired balloon, with pastor and pilot
     as witnesses, cross the bay's south shore, and land
In a green ball field of a private school, on the rich
     peninsula. They would drive back down

And start life. Mama should be lying wide awake, dressed,
  on her day bed. No longer
Queen of the mobile home, all melon rind and pulp, a truth
  about Kentucky. Now,
Twenty years later, she was a stick of hanging flesh,
  topped with a red scarf to hide
The scarred bald head. Iris saw the empty bed and nearly
  called for Smith, and stopped.
All these years—the phrase repeated in the hollow of her
  throat. These years
With Mama absent/present, a human secret. Ruth said, "She's
  out for a walk," and grabbed
Iris by the wrist, pulling her back from going out the door,
  and passing her
To leave herself. "Don't miss the lunch." She watched
  her daughter, businesslike and happy, leave,
And saw that, just like that, her leaving, her going out
  the door this Saturday morning, ended
Life with her mother and grandmother. Iris looked back
  into the house, her poet's voice
Rode over the man's snoring back in their room. It spoke
  of emblems—his, the rock and hawk,
Conjoined in noble meaning. Iris shook her head and felt
  the eardrums bend. No time
For revery, for listening to the voice that kept her company,
  it, too, muffled by years—
Jeffers' voice, talking of a life she could not keep from
  haunting her. No time.
Her mama must be out there, haunting the esplanade, or
  looking into someone's window—
One of those tinted picture windows made to frame a
  Pacific sunset and block out

Any who shuffled past and would peer in. Outside, the
    morning overcast, that always
Looked permanent but burned away by afternoon. A bird
    that color stitched
And needled through an olive tree. A car went down the
    street, its bareness—no tree bigger
Than a fruit tree, wide apart—always a quick reminder.
    This was not home.
The eucalyptus trees, those Australians her poet planted
    in his poems, keeping
Their distance, green-black heads, wind or heat warped,
    stood blocks away, like clouds on the horizon.
Behind the house the grape arbor was empty, a port of
    cobwebs. The neighbor's magnolia
Standing behind the shake fence full of open cups of
    blossom—not a stranger.
She'd known them in Kentucky. She had written her name
    in thumbnail on the fleshy petals,
Watching it turn brown as antique ink. She ran the two
    blocks to the beach, taking
The lawn's dew on her bare feet, printing a few squares
    of white sidewalk, and stopped at the cliff edge.
The surfers were afloat in waiting shallows. They looked
    as if they'd climbed, like new cicadas,
Out of the earth of water up these gravestones, the tipped
    boards poking up they held on to.
There was the cloud-gray surface of the sea, a face like
    Mama's face, that TV-stare.
If Mama knew things, like a patient in a coma who can hear,
    she knew Ruth's plans.
When Iris took her outside for a walk, she'd follow like
    a bicycle, guided,

Keeping pace without will. Yet dressed herself, did her
  bathroom business, chose TV shows.
Iris ran back, then past the schoolyard to the highway.
  Cars waited at lights. This highway
Went north and had she ever taken it? The ice cream
  stand was brewing its first coffee.
The surfers would arrive soon. Mama liked the ice cream.
  At the end—or what she could
Imagine as the highway's end—her poet's house, the house
  he had built himself
Of stones rolled from the sea, waited for her to come
  up to the door, knock, and ask, "Have you
Seen an old lady in a red bandana? She's from Kentucky.
  She was made crazy
By a shotgun blast that scalped her and also by the murder
  of her lover and her sons. There's more—
But I'm pressed for time." Iris walked back, aware her
  feet were bruised from running.
One toe bled. She squatted to the paper in the yard. She
  went inside and heard Smith's
Wave-slosh in the bathroom. Mama was gone. All these years.
  A hummingbird found sunlight
At the kitchen window feeder, enough to set it flaming,
  a digit scribbling fire,
And sped away. Iris thought of salmon finding their way
  up rivers, of new souls
Weighed down by guilt or buoyed by innocence, finding their
  places after death.

After Smith left the house, to sit inside his bar, alone,
  until the wedding lunch,

Iris dressed and stood before the bathroom mirror and
  tried to read herself. She saw
A face no more responsive than the leaden likeness of her
  poet on his book.
His face looked from the paperback through stains and creases,
  eyes focused inward, or
Sizing up a boulder, comparing it with some niche ready in
  his tower—
That look that both extends and feeds back in. She gave
  herself that look, a lean dry woman
In middleage, the hardened lines of inward living and out-
  ward skepticism softened
By downy hairs, like a boy's peach fuzz. She heard her poet
  talking to the Trojan prophetess,
Cassandra, comparing himself to her. "You and I, Cassandra,"
  his last comment.
He spoke of how truth-telling like his own and hers disgusted
  men and gods, but Iris
Wanted to hear him say the same to her, "Iris, you and I,"
  for other reasons.
Dressed, she would have time to call the police, then drive
  slowly through the neighborhood.
Ruth was right. Mama was out walking. She must know
  something. Iris would find her.
She hooked an earring on, leaning as if to listen to the
  mirror speak, and heard
The back door open and a voice begin to talk. She found
  a woman in the kitchen,
A white-haired, worried stranger with an ancient-looking
  tan in a flowered mu mu.
"I've seen an older lady sitting in your backyard," she
  said, then spoke in tumbling fragments.

"I live behind. You know an old lady? Sits in your
    lanai? I just came running.
I've seen her here, in your lanai. From my yard, through
    the fence. I came right over." "My mother,"
Iris said. "You've seen my mother?" "Yes," the woman said.
    "I've seen her here." "I mean
This morning," Iris said. "She has been missing." The
    woman swallowed, like an excited child,
Gasping before she spoke. "Something has happened," she
    said. "I think." They hurried around the block,
The frightened woman in the mu mu hustling ahead. Iris
    stopped to pull off her high heels,
Then found that she was counting sidewalk squares and
    skipping lines to spare her mother's spine.
They ran into the onshore breeze then turned south, then
    turned up the block. "She's here," the woman said.
A stucco house, adobe style, like theirs. The woman pushed
    a gate of redwood shakes
Open across the gravel path beside the house, the rust
    complaining in its hinges.
"Right here," she said. The big magnolia whose leaves
    Iris had admired behind their house,
Whose sheen reminded her of home, stood above its rusty
    trash of fallen leaves
And Mama, nestled among them in the tree's shadow. "I
    don't think she's dead," the woman whispered,
More to herself than Iris, but gasped when Iris said,
    "My God. Oh, God." "I'm sure she isn't dead,"
The woman pleaded. "Oh, my God. My God," said Iris,
    tearing both her nylons
To kneel beside her mother, curled and soft and furred
    with wet grime, like a dead cat, the bandana

74

Gone, and her scalp, a cap of scars, sprinkled with sparse
    gray hairs. She was face down in the leaves,
Her hands drawn up between her breasts. "My mama's dead,"
    said Iris. "My God," her neighbor said.

At the wedding lunch, when food was served and sat before
    each guest and received the benediction
From Reverend Sarton, of the Kiwanis Club, and the comments
    on how good it looked,
Iris endeavored to depict her poet in her mind, pointing
    aloft to the stars
Or out to sea, palming a stone and gazing at it like a
    crystal ball and saying,
"Here is the only future worth anticipating." No use.
    She looked at her place,
The steaming loaf of chicken, the parallel lengths of string
    beans, the yellow grains of rice,
The water glass, the glass of greenish wine, the shiny
    roll, the pat of pallid butter,
The heavy-looking silverware, and knew that, soon, she
    had to turn again to speak
To Mrs. Sarton, Richard's mother, and Ruth's mother-in-
    law to be, and not mention
How her own mother was at that minute lying on the couch
    at home, laid out
Where Iris and her neighbor had ensconced her, struggling,
    having driven her back around
The block and hefted her into the house (a younger Mama
    would have been more trouble),
And tried to make her comfortable. She had told Ruth that
    Mama wouldn't leave the TV—

75

A sudden stubbornness, caused, perhaps, by knowing what
     was happening. Ruth understood.
Now Iris sat, trying to make an effort and not count the
     glasses of green wine
Smith gulped like soda pop. His fez hung on his chair back.
     Was human beauty—
As her poet said it was—unbearable unless the heart was
     hardened? She looked
At Mrs. Sarton and regarded strength and weakness of the
     heart in the dark lips
And the blue stain on the lower one, and a ripeness unlike
     Mama's blowzy prime
Those years back in the mobile home, but a yielding to the
     bone. She smiled, and her teeth shone,
White and hard, between the bluish lips. The smile
     encouraged Iris and the full flesh
Of the woman's arms spoke of love for children. Nothing
     like that in the Reverend Sarton.
His scrubbed hair was plastered to his skull, his nose
     a pigeon beak. He had ingested
A squad of pills poured out beside his water glass and
     listened now to Smith, his lips
Compressed into a thread, his knife and fork poised at
     his chicken kiev. Smith was too drunk
To care or notice that the cleric looked at him as if
     he was a brief encounter
With embarrassment. Smith told his shaggy dog story,
     requiring a response
Every few seconds from the hungry preacher. Sarton kept
     his knife and fork in the air,
Answering Smith's questions about the story line, then
     thrust them in his food.

A stream of seasoned butter sprayed his glasses. Across
   the table, sitting beside Ruth's maid of honor,
Richard inclined his head to her and whispered and smiled
   and she leaned back to laugh,
Stretching her torso, swelling breasts, then setting to her
   food again, both of them—Ruth, too—
Alight with that amusement at the world, that feeling
   (How long had Iris sensed
Its absence?) that the world was understandable and not
   so serious—a free-for-all.
Her brothers died believing it, that the world wished you
   well, once you had joined it. A lie!
But could you hold that feeling all your life, surely
   it would become a truth. The glass
In Richard's hand exploded. Wine soaked the table and
   the pretty maid of honor. Blood
Appeared, but just as quickly her future son-in-law had
   wrapped his hand inside a napkin,
And tried to mop the wine that soaked the table and the
   girl. Only Iris seemed concerned.
Not Mr. or Mrs. Sarton. Smith was drunk. And Ruth, talking
   to the best man, offered
Her napkin, too. "It's nerves," said Mrs. Sarton. "Ricky
   gets so nervous he breaks things.
At home he drinks from metal tumblers." Iris saw the
   leaded crystal stemware, the gift
From her and Smith, shattering glass by glass in the young
   man's grip and Ruth
Mopping up wine and blood and bandaging his hand. The
   waiter brought a new glass. Richard,
Not touching it, shrugged an apology, and went on joking
   with the bridesmaid.

A long faced, Gallic boy, with wheaten skin, his mother's
　　smile, nothing from his father.
Iris thought, "Oh, well," and said for no one else to hear,
　　"I wonder if he can bend keys
With his mind?" The silliness relaxed her, made her smile.
　　"Or raise the dead?"

Was Ruth a woman that a man would build a tower for, like
　　Jeffers' Una—heroic, untamed,
As he described his wife, like one in a ballad? Iris looked
　　across the table, wondering.
This child was her age now, when twenty years ago, past
　　midnight, with sudden animal fear,
Iris put her and Mama into the truck and drove west
　　sixty hours. Was Iris a girl then,
As Ruth now seemed to her? She hadn't felt like one
　　nor did she think she was a woman
A poet would erect an edifice of boulders for or write
　　a poem in praise of.
Perhaps, this child would be or could be. The round face,
　　high cheekbones, and happy eyes
That danced, eager to please, on either tip of the smile,
　　or popped with anger—no,
They lacked solemnity or tragedy. But there was stead-
　　fastness to match her name,
And pity, too, compassion for another's misery—things
　　Iris had hoped for when
She named her. Or had naming Ruth been Iris's own wish for
　　steadfastness and pity? Leaving her husband
(Whose face regarded her from Ruth's eyes, whose addictions
　　Ruth translated into love),

Fleeing to California and now, estranged from the one who
   saved her yet remaining,
Was this like Ruth the heroine? It was not. It was another
   story of survival.
And like such tales its mood was ruthlessness. The look
   Ruth gave her back when she saw Iris
Did not say, "I know what you have been through" or "We
   two will never be divided."
But only, "Mother, I am happy at this moment. Please,
   let me stay that way."
The boy that she would marry offered kindness and humor,
   with a little nervousness.
But darting glances at Smith and Reverend Sarton, this
   pair of fathers, Ruth conveyed
His difference and her look was changed from one of warning
   to a gaze of sympathy.
She had her beauty; that would be enough. And Iris saw
   that endurance made them sisters.
A knife rapped out a tune on someone's glass. The best
   man rose to make a toast.
It was enough then—Iris couldn't help but see it was—to
   be her daughter's sister.

The fan spun air into the nylon bag of the balloon, laid
   out in the parking lot
Of Reverend Sarton's church. The faintest onshore breeze
   cut through the heat; on the hottest days,
If you stood still you'd feel that constant motion shore-
   ward, as if the urge of waves to break
Released the spirit of their movement and it continued,
   dying in the slightest breath

Of moisture, cool and salty. It was hot. The thermal
    draft would lift them high across the bay.
Yet Iris felt that trace of salty coolness on her cheeks
    and watched the pilot work
To lift his great balloon erect with the propane engine's
    blast of heat. Ruth had told her
That rising in a hot air balloon straight up was like a
    resurrection; Iris believed her.
She had herself lifted her daughter up away from death,
    but as a mother cat
Mouths a kitten in its fangs and picks it off the floor.
    To rise below
A colored sack of heated air had no appeal for Iris. All
    her life the religious
Had been attained through horizontal movement. Flight
    was escape, and rescue and escape
Were Iris's religion. Aiming west three nights with child
    and mother, reading straight
Into her poet's heart, which she saw as part boulder and
    part wave—or as the print
Of breaking water bedded into rock, a headlong motion not
    a rising thought.
Even Smith's response to life as their poor savior was
    to take it lying down, drunk and broke.
But if for Ruth to rise below an engine roaring fire into
    a massive windbreaker,
To float above the lacy nets and ha ha's of the shorebreak,
    rising up the cliffs,
To land in some green meadow among the roofs of wealthy
    houses was like a resurrection,
Then, so be it. She watched as Ruth, her groom, the pilot,
    and the Reverend Sarton rose

From the parking lot. She drove along the esplanade
    toward the landing place. The balloon,
A garlic bulb of colors, ascending over the blue and shifting
    water, carried the ceremony,
The ritual that Ruth and Richard had made up for each
    other, in its gondola.
Beautiful to observe, curious to note the silent drifting,
    then to hear the roar
As the pilot fired the engine and its flame shot into
    the lifting emptiness.

Now a few words on the narrowness of fate, on tragedy in
    the small—a view,
Not of the massive comber thrust against the cliff face
    time and again, and the huge result
That stares out, ravaged, through a veil of mist, but
    of the backwash running down the beach
To turn tail out to sea, slapping against the breaker
    with a pop. A word about
The glass embedded in the shallows' rippled floor, the
    deep sea fish that swims too close
And slips into a tide pool, caught, as the tide ebbs,
    a view of nature's imperfections,
Those human analogues, reduced for the sake of understanding,
    to shells churned up by storm surf.
Small on the crumbling sea cliffs, silhouetted with their
    poles against the foaming beach break,
Leaving eroding tracks that fill with water from below,
    stooping to claw behind
The sand flea disappearing in the soaked muck, the
    electrified, pathetic—

They feel the cliff give way, the surge up-end their child,
   the handshake of the lightning climb
Their arm, and their appeal is to nothing that nature
   understands. They cry for mercy.
The trail that any wary creature travels by its instinct,
   they call grace, and when
They stray they ask for mercy. Nothing else does. There
   are protests, but never prayers.

Home from the wedding, Iris entered the quiet house and
   saw her mother, resting
Where she had left her on the sofa, stretched out as if
   to nap, a fresh bandana knotted
Around her head, her head indenting a small pillow, her
   two hands placed upon her chest
As Iris placed her own hands before sleep, one atop the
   other on her breastbone.
The house dress grimy still, crushed leaf bits clinging
   here and there, but her face wiped clean,
As white as Ivory Soap, even seeming to float a little,
   like a cake of Ivory,
Upon the dim air of the living room. Protected by its
   northern exposure, the room
Stayed cool when there was no Santana wind. Standing
   in it now, Iris thought she could be anywhere—
Under the double hedgeapples, in spring, before the summer
   onslaught of the heat,
In the Kentucky mobile home, herself returned with Ruth,
   four years old, her husband's
Bruises still tender on her ribs, her mother irritated
   at the big surprise.

No, there was never such tranquillity in that house as
　　there was now—right now—in this.
She put a kettle on for tea, laid out a t-shirt and a
　　pair of jeans, and changed.
Back in the kitchen, she almost called out, "Mama, would
　　you like a cup of tea?" A question
Mama would not have answered if she were alive. For
　　twenty years, she'd answered nothing.
And Iris caught herself and thought, "She's napping."
　　And caught herself again—backwash, embedded
Splinter of glass—"That's right. She's dead." Iris
　　sat down and drank her cup of tea, beside
Her mother. She'd said nothing at Ruth's wedding. Waiting
　　in the ball field of the school,
Overlooking the bay, the wedding guests had watched how the
　　slow balloon ascended toward them,
Then rose above the screen of eucalyptus, and angled its
　　descent right to their feet.
The gondola touched down in centerfield and skipped a
　　few steps, giddily. Champagne
Was poured in plastic flutes. And someone honked his
　　car horn. Reverend Sarton, helped to the ground,
Muttered to his wife that once was enough, but shook
　　his son's hand, kissed Ruth, and took Iris's hand
In both of his own, unsteady, and a little pale. For him
　　the flight was not religious,
Unless he'd recognized the shock of the soul's flight after
　　death. Iris could see a gaiety
In Ruth's eyes that she'd never known herself, a deep
　　and private pleasure that she'd never known
Was gaiety. And Richard swaggered like a homerun king,
　　holding the plastic flute,

And talking, laughing, taking more champagne, the glass
    remaining intact in his grip.
Iris told Ruth goodbye. The joy in Ruth's eyes held its
    deep composure. For a moment,
Iris felt it, too, a shaft of inner life where she could
    hear two voices talking—
Her poet's voice and hers. She smiled and saw Ruth's
    tears and felt her own. And now she raised
The teacup to her lips and looked down at Mama. The
    north light showed
The coils of rising steam, like smoke transmuted from
    the tea's dark surface. A small thing.

The moon looked through the chain link gate behind Smith's
    warehouse and showed the keyhole in the padlock
And the key wavering in Smith's hand while Smith, one
    eye closed, tried to fit it like a thread
Into a needle's eye. The moon was candid and not as sorry
    as the man was for himself.
It did not turn away as he had, when the wedding ended,
    from Iris, from himself.
He had turned backwards in himself so that he didn't have
    to watch. But the moon saw
His struggle to lift up the swinging gate. She watched
    his belly work against the metal frame,
Forelock of oiled hair dislodge, the sweat start. He
    had decided to burn everything.
And the solvent moonlight marked most everything that
    he would burn. The warehouse, oddly lit,
Looked like a grade school being cleaned at night, haunted
    by an adult sweeping up

The remains of childhood. Smith had looked ahead to being
   that success he was near forty,
Some twenty years before—a life of giving beer and tanning
   lotion to grateful strangers.
Now, he was a man dressed for a wedding, inflated by debt
   and booze and worry, preparing
To save his skin by torching it, to slough it like a sunburn.
   Burn it all. And give
Money to the women—Iris, Ruth, the mother—make them happy
   and then leave.
Pick up where he left off. He chose a paperback he recog-
   nized from a boxful
And started on a sex scene, 'fifties porn, the sex all
   mental, in the talk—before
And after—and in metaphors of bodies like quicksilver,
   the woman hissing, "Don't
Tease me," hard nipples, corded male arms, thighs described
   by qualities of smoothness, parting.
Feel sorry for the arsonist E. Smith, walking to his office
   to find matches,
Engrossed in a dirty book. But praise her willing counter-
   thrust, his gentle but commanding
Way with her, as she supports his weight. Praise his patience
   and control. Smith groped,
The book still at his nose, in drawers, on shelves, under
   the paperweight—the .45.
Now praise the climax. Hers. His. And Smith, as if
   accidents do happen perfectly,
As he leaves the past and leaps into the present. The
   book shouts. Its pages fly and spin.
And on the floor at Smith's feet, the gun, the paperweight
   automatic, lies where he has knocked it,

Dribbling smoke, having aimed exactly at the spine of
   Whispered Passions. Smith holds his breath
And sits straight in his desk chair. A last page swings
   down past his face. He looks up at the ceiling,
Feels his head. An oracle has spoken. He must go home.
   He must burn nothing, let
The gasoline and moonlight dry from newspapers and rags
   throughout the warehouse, and go home.
No pausing in the drive, no turning back. Inside the house
   he finds the women, the live one and the dead,
And hears, before his voice can speak the words, Iris
   saying, "I think it's time to go."

III

Now, she was free, as free as all her ghosts—the ghost
    of Cale, a devil of white dust,
Whirled by a sobbing voice that begged for money;
    the ghosts of Rice and Hoy like Toby jugs,
Glazed with their gleaming sweat, brimful of cheery
    brew, their skulls blown open at the top;
Mama's friend Charles, a smiling nodding ghost, a stalk
    of yellow corn smutted with gunpowder;
Mama, poor Mama, in her red bandana, like a dead cat
    under the magnolia,
The ghost of absence. Smith, her own great crime, puzzled
    an act of kindness should explode
And lodge him in a life he would have lived by choice and
    lived more happily.
And Ruth, an apparition drifting off, from wave to cloud-
    less sky, and out of reach,
The direction she'd been heading all her life. And what
    was Iris now herself? A ghost,
Haunting a life she imagined from a book of poems by a
    poet who was dead,
And a living woman, too, free to drive north to make the
    pilgrimage she had dreamed of,
Taking the coast road, watching the ocean take on wilder
    angles, dipping out of view,
Then rising between wind-planed coastal hills where trees
    showed the warp of the great pressure
Applied by all that motion from the west, under the guise
    of peace. She was so free,
She thought she could surrender daydreaming, the tacking
    drift that threw her in the way
Of kitchen traffic, knife blades, broken glass, the every-
    day disasters dreamers pass through

Like air until air turns to steel or stone. She saw the
    hitchhikers, commune survivors
And leftovers from hardluck logging camps, sitting on
    suitcases or, backs to the traffic,
Walking with thumb turned forward as if breasting, one-armed,
    through chest-deep water, or standing still with signs,
Nicknaming cities. She imagined that she chose one, and
    found a hand around her throat,
Both of them hidden on a bank of lupine, by the road.
    There he lay beside her, hearing
Her heart race underneath his hand, and said with cruel
    amazement, how fast it beat; and she,
Head turned away on the crushed bed of wildflowers,
    answered, "It is because I fear for my life."
She gripped the wheel and cursed and shook herself for
    cursing at a daydream, and asked
Why she would make herself a victim in a fantasy. Whose
    hand had she imagined?
She hissed at her desire to be created out of words. If
    Jeffers could create her,
He would look with his fastidious distaste on her humanity,
    yet pity her
In her distress and, if she could respond with her own
    violence, he would admire her.
And then, she knew she had been making sure the figure
    up ahead, walking slowly,
Was who she thought, in army coat, fat jeans, backpack,
    floppy stetson and loops of hair—
A woman. Not the first that she had seen, but first
    alone, and could her day-nightmare
Have risen when she saw the distant shape? Or was she
    stopping now because her own

Imagination veered her into trouble? The hitchhiker—
   who hadn't signaled for a ride—
Reached out to take the door handle as naturally as a hand
   goes down to stroke a faithful dog.
She folded into the front seat like a storm cloud, crackling
   with phlegm, stinking of tobacco,
Her sack of a body drowned in the sack of her clothes,
   all khaki flaps and pockets with fresh packs
Of cigarettes and flattened ones in crumpled membranous
   sheaths and, under the coat, the swaddling
Of an old sweater, loose-knit purple wool, drooping in
   gaping stitches over her breasts
And belly. She wore a man's white shirt, the unbuttoned
   collar corners limp as a cat's handshake.
She settled down in the gray cloud of her scent and Iris
   nearly asked her, as she might
Enquire about another woman's fragrance (knowing that she
   would never learn the truth),
Just what it was, not only cigarettes or sweat, but a faint
   odor of out-of-doors,
From hours of walking outside in the breath—so Iris
   thought—of ocean breezes.
Before the woman spoke, she grabbed the ashtray's lip,
   pulled out a flattened cigarette,
And lit up with a paper match. Iris said, "I don't mind."
   The hitchhiker cracked the window
And aimed a plume of smoke there, bringing forth a cough
   that she sucked back.
The car hummed and the woman added to it a buzz of mumbling,
   as if her inner voice
Were barely audible. Iris watched the road and noticed
   when she studied her companion

She did not glance back but held her forward-looking stare,
    knowing that Iris looked at her.
The highway dipped and rose, revealing waves unfolding,
    folding, made of glass or smashed
Into white water. The coastal swell and breaking of the
    landscape mirrored the waves.
What did you talk about with such a stranger? She felt
    a burning band of sweat begin
Across her forehead, the sign that she was failing some
    important test. Her stomach fell
And slowed her, but she leaned to pick up speed. And then
    a mystery evaporated.
She knew the woman's scent, a morning air, forgotten all
    these years. Out of the folds
Of the hitchhiker's clothes an earth smell emanated—the
    perfume of ploughed fields, earth ready
To be planted in. "How far are you going?" Iris asked.
    The woman smiled
And showed a slice of cracked teeth webbed with stains.
    Her stream of inner conversation ceased.
"I'll go as far as you go," she responded, and grinned,
    and the private speech began again.

Iris remembered the damp Kentucky fall, the crayon-
    colored leaves, the slick ply, one
By one, of thousands of them smothering the land, on
    asphalt, windowsills, and doorsteps,
On roofs of cars, chrome yellow, rust, hiding the painted
    steel, all beauties of dying. Rising,
A creature of dead leaves, a damp autumn-figure, reached
    out crumbling hands

To take her back. She blinked and shivered; the overcast
   bled gouts of gluttonous fog, no leaves
Turned on the trees—live oak and eucalyptus. She had
   to quell this inner melodrama
And tried to recollect how Jeffers mourned his wife's
   death. "Beautiful years when she was by me,"
He wrote, and as if the shoreline read her mind, it
   appeared again with the rock at Morro Bay.
Her passenger was keeping herself company, droning layered
   monologues
That darkened like obsidian. She had to part the voices
   and pulled over. The rock
Stood like a city of medieval birds, an allegory in
   contemporary
Haze and angled evening sunlight, coming through a cloud-
   break. To embody grief, Jeffers
Described a lowtide with its stinking seaweed and beached
   fishing boats. But Iris could see
A table of gray-silver water in an aureole of twilit mist,
   the rock,
Rising with pale cliffs, cowled in gray-green vegetation,
   and the bird flocks—multitudinous,
All colors between white and black, the whiter ones
   arising from the tidal flats,
Making great tours around the cliff faces and settling in
   niches; the darker ones already
Fixed like contemplatives, heads bowed in prayer. Jeffers
   spoke of rattlesnakes,
"Stored lightnings in the stone cloud," and admonished
   them to guard the rock. But who would want
To live in such an otherworldly place, among thick bird
   clusters? A hermit?

Content to live alone so close to shore, on this chunk
     of continent, with gulls to feed him.
They sat in the car, Iris and the huddled woman talking
     to herself, until,
No longer able to maintain her focus on the rock or what
     her poet wrote,
Iris said ruefully, nearly laughing, "What? Say that
     again." Then, she did laugh.
"'Beautiful years when she was by me,'" Iris quoted aloud and
     looked at the strange woman, a gaze
She felt would counteract her irony with pity, and started
     the car again. This time
The woman paused and said to Iris, "What?" And Iris
     smiled and said, "No, you tell me."
The highway cut against the bakebrown cliffs, the foxtail
     fields on one side, and the ocean,
That seemed to stand for all that was peripheral, falling
     away on the other, yet
There, always, like an idea of absence or of presence,
     withdrawing and attending, glinting.
Iris inclined her head to hear her passenger. She leaned
     and held her pose, determined
To know what her fellow pilgrim had to say, still looking
     straight ahead to mind the road,
The way when her daughter was a child and rode beside her
     she'd listen to her speak. This road
She knew would follow the coastline that her poet loved
     and end, for her, at his doorstep.
Already she'd stopped listening, hearkening instead to her
     own inner voices. She leaned,
Smiled, listened, looking straight ahead. Above them,
     on the right, a hawk went gliding sideways.

Gulls, on the left, dashed out of sight to the rock shore.
    The woman shrank from Iris, then leaned
Toward her, chin out. "You won't get rid of me that easy,"
    she said. Iris couldn't answer,
But watched her work a cigarette out of a fresh pack and
    thought she recognized
Something of her own unloved Kentucky in the jutting jaw,
    the lipless mouth,
The eyes that warily regarded the lit match and the stranger
    studying her face.
"Before I ever saw the ocean," Iris said and saw the woman
    cock her head
To light the cigarette and listen, too. "Like people who
    have never been to it,
I'd seen a lot of pictures and I'd read about it. My images
    lacked something—
The feel of it, not just the water but the air of it,
    the part that you can grab
And ask a question. Before I ever saw it face to face,
    I knew when I did see it,
I'd have an answer to a question. Not in so many words
    or in some flight of gulls
Or sandpipers or shape of washed-up kelp. The question
    wasn't in so many words.
And I don't think it was about the sea. I wonder if
    I ever got an answer."
Now Iris thought of how her poet said it, describing
    the Pacific, "the hill of water."
He made it more rhetorical than that; "this dome, this
    half-globe, this bulging eyeball,"
He wrote, and stated that it did not watch "our wars."
    What did it watch? That one word, "hill,"—

It made it seem so homely; you could climb a hill and
    look back where you lived, your house . . .
And now the passenger put out her cigarette and touched
    Iris lightly on the forearm,
As if she knew this gesture was enough to wake her. And
    Iris flinched, afraid she'd slept
While driving, and gripped the wheel, and blinked, and
    said, "Yes? What? Was I asleep?" "My name is Nora,"
The woman said. "I used to walk down to the shore at
    dawn and wait to see a man
Who came there, too, to feed the seals. The fog would
    lift around him, coming from the point.
He was always there before me. He had a sailor's duffel
    full of day old bread. The gulls
Would swoop like crazy angels round his shoulders. His
    beard was green, with shells and seaweed in it."
Iris began to draw in breath to let out in a kind, indulgent
    sigh. The woman heard her.
"Wait," she said. And continued with her story. How the
    old man never stopped to talk. How once
She brought her own stale bread and walked into the fog
    bank on the point and found the seals,
Emerging from the pewter-colored water, waiting to be
    fed. And so she'd fed them.
Then, as the gray veils lifted, gulls came down, circling
    her, beaks parting, snapping for the bread.
She couldn't toss it to them fast enough. "One cut my
    scalp," she said, and pulled her hat off,
Showing the dark tongue sticking down the scalp into the
    brow. Iris glanced at it.
And Jeffers' lines came back and filled her heart: "I
    have seen strange things in my time . . . a merman

Standing waist deep in the ocean off my rock-shore. Un-
    mistakably human and unmistakably
A sea-beast: he submerged and never came up again . . .
    I do not know what he was . . . but this
Was the least of wonders." The poetry arose from Nora's
    story, and Iris realized
Her breath was thinning; she would have to think of breathing
    for a moment to calm down.
"The poet Jeffers," she asked Nora. "Have you heard of him?"
"I might have," Nora said.

Night started at the red bead of the sunset, an eye of
    magma, draining from a funnel.
The cone of darkness widened through the hues of twilight,
    the grades of deepening blue. Headlights
And stars came on; the former hugged the sheer cliffs
    of the highway; the latter clung to the wheel
That cranked the moon in place over the Santa Lucias
    and then above the expanse of ocean.
The moonlight fell, a blob of mercury that shattered
    across the water's wrinkled skin.
Iris did not intend to stop until Carmel, until she'd
    made her pilgrimage.
Talking, even if only to herself aloud (she'd spent a
    lifetime doing it in silence),
Would keep her awake. This time, unlike all times before,
    she thought she had a listener.
But in the dark Iris couldn't tell if Nora slept or
    listened, waiting.
Her idling undertone of speech that harmonized with the
    car's ongoing thrum had stopped.

"Sometimes I like to think," Iris began, "that I am living a
    life I've read about."
Nora said nothing, but her silence against the car door
    was like an ear.
Iris remembered a passage Una Jeffers had written. The
    stars went over
The lonely ocean—no, in this condition, driving through
    the night up Highway One,
There was no loneliness. She saw herself arriving, and
    at the same time, in Una's words,
She looked south from the headland where the house stood,
    Tor House, that Una's husband built for her.
She could see, beyond the Carmel River's mouth, the gentle
    rounded outlines of the mountains—
The Santa Lucias—bright green with pasture, dark with
    chaparral and sage. There was a scar
Of yellow ivory that marked a quarry where Indians had
    hewed out blocks of chalkstone
To build the Spanish mission. The mountains, serenely
    lovely, turned magnificent, menacing faces
Toward the sea. The river, too, appeared serene; except,
    in winter, floods raged down
The valley, surged through new-cut channels, and collided
    with the waves across the sand bar.
At most times it spread out, a placid lake, and trickled
    into adjacent water meadows.
Among the tough grasses, reeds, the changing hues of sky and
    cloud were mirrored, with dark hill shadows.
Wild swans and ducks and geese, local herons, egrets
    passing, rested there and fed.
Birds filled the air with song. Over sand spits, by
    open water, gulls fished and swirled;

Their white wings flashed. Before a storm they floated
   high aloft for hours, weaving circles
Of some precise but complicated ritual. The coast road
   crossed the river and headed
South (Up this road Iris took her traveller and her story).
   Mountains hurried
In great cliffs to the sea; slashed by canyons, only rarely
   did they flatten to ploughland—
A possible few acres. Cattle left the welts of centuries
   of hoof tracks across
The steep hillsides. And in the canyons, crowding the springs
   and streams, the trees thrived—redwoods and pines,
Laurels and tan oaks, maples, sycamores, and high up,
   with manzanita in their shadows,
The rosy barked madrone. Down near the Little Sur River,
   dunes would cross the road. Beyond,
The Point Sur lighthouse topped its rock, like a sea gull
   perched for nightfall, three hundred feet
Above the sea. Its beam and siren warned of broken ships,
   of mile and mile of shore,
Jagged with sharp cliffs, narrow inlets, rare furlongs of
   white beach no one could climb down to.
The lashing waves rolled in, a green and blue beyond belief,
   beyond the foam, and in storm,
A grim cathedral color, full of judgment. Iris knew she
   might have only darkness
For a listener. But she remembered Una's catalog of colors
   and wished she could
Reach over and touch Nora, but she held the wheel and put
   her faith in Nora's silence.
She told about the flowers around Tor House, the blues of
   lupine and wild lilac, iris,

Larkspur and blue-eyed grass; the gold of poppies, yellow
    lupine, wild pansies, wall-flowers,
The whiteness of white heather, white wild lilac. Then
    the flashing colors of the birds.
The red winged blackbirds darting from their posts to
    flare their shoulders; gold finches and all kinds
Of emerald and red in hummingbirds. And high above,
    the subtler colors of hawks,
Their arrogance and hovering, marsh hawks and sparrow
    hawks, red tails, peregrine falcons.
Black sails of vultures with their small heads peering
    downward. And even on sunny days, a wisp
Of sea-gray fog, luminous, vagrant, creeping like a live
    thing in and out of canyons.
It was the spirit of abandonment, Iris believed, that drew
    both the Jeffers. The ruins
Of a deserted farm, old cart wheels, antique gear, a
    caved-in well; to take in hand
Forgotten calico rags that fell apart, or to start at
    calla lilies, flourishing, cold,
From shining leaves. Old saw mills, a landing where great
    loads of redwood once went out on ships.
The coal mine, just a hump of thistles, where the twenty
    Chinese workmen lost their lives.
"I know," said Iris, "just how they would make an exploration."
    She said it like a proposal
To see if Nora would object. The car responded with its
    unchanging motion. Nora
Let Iris see her face, when she looked over. She was
    listening. "Perhaps," thought Iris,
"Waiting her turn," and smiled and accelerated slightly
    and began. "Late afternoon,"

Said Iris, "and they were starting back, along a stream
   where pastures opened up and walls
Of canyon rock pressed close." (All she could make for
   them to travel through was what she'd read.)
"Robin walked with a stick of manzanita. Una had Haig,
   the bulldog, on a leash.
The great green steps of pasture were scored in half
   by shadow, and shadow drowned the narrow passes.
Beef cattle in small groups stood at a distance, out
   of the sun, ruminating, pointing
West as they were. They, too, preferred the shadow half,
   and Una let the bulldog free
To run in and out of sun and shade. Ahead they saw a
   squarish, half-green, medusa shape,
A box of dying vines that had been a shack, a hairy house
   collapsing in the grip
Of poison oak. It wasn't such a strange sight for the
   place. The matting of the vines
Was up to two feet thick, and through a slit they saw
   the inside, too, where pale dead leaves
Clung like 3D wallpaper and carpeting. Nothing else
   inside. They walked on.
But places like that shack were portents of abandonment,
   and soon they found a house,
Deserted where the stream flowed through a stand of redwoods;
   new growth pushed through walls; inside,
They saw the sapling tops coming up through floors. The
   dried out putty of the windows dropped
The panes like leaves. All was dim as in a gothic sanctuary.
   The dirty glass
Of the remaining window panes and the clean spaces where
   the glass was gone let in

The gloomy half-light, tinged by the red color of the
    tree trunks. The still nailed floor boards
That forest hadn't tilted out of place bled moisture
    with each step; one sprang, when Robin
Put a foot down, revealing nails at one end—rusty fangs.
    An open door swung shut—
Imagine all the years of tensile balance and the first
    human step to interrupt it—
And then they saw the portrait in its simple frame, the
    old fashioned crayon enlargement, hidden
Where even this cathedral twilight couldn't fade it,
    forgotten in the move, perhaps,
Because behind the door, or put there on purpose, to
    forget. It moved them both to see it.
It was a portrait of a woman, not yet old but old fashioned—
    prim around the mouth,
And laced up primly to her throat, her hair pinned close,
    her eyes—rather her gaze—elsewhere.
You couldn't make her eyes out, but they didn't look
    beyond the picture plane; they looked
Inward. It was the look of someone who would have been
    content to stand behind a door
For decades, generations." Iris halted. She had been
    driving slowly, but the talking
Had slowed her even more. Now headlights of a string
    of cars—some five or six—behind her
Glared back from her rear view. She pulled over and
    let the cars speed past; one blew its horn.

Nora started talking to herself or to someone who looked
    back from the windshield,

Perhaps the line of pent-up cars, unwinding now up the
cliffside road ahead. She was pleading.
"Open this door," she said. "You open it right now!"
She made her body straighten, shudder.
Now Iris did reach over; beneath her hand—she lay it
on Nora's shoulder—the woman trembled
And her coat felt damp. Nora was shouting now, "They
won't let me out!" She grabbed the dashboard.
"I'll let you out," said Iris. "But it's dark. Do you
want to get out on the road like this?"
The rigid anguish went out of her with a sigh. "No," said
Nora. "No, I want to stay."
Iris pulled back onto the road and leaned ahead, forcing
power through the engine.
The story of the woman's crayon portrait dwindled behind,
waiting, as she had
Behind the door, to be picked up again. And now as if
she knew that Iris felt
The need to drive and not speak, Nora said, "I'm going
home. I wasn't going,
Till you picked me up. Now, I've decided to." Iris held
even stiller, tense on the wheel,
And tried to control her breathing like the forward motion
of the car, to make
A hush to camouflage her heedfulness, lest she scare the
speaker into incoherence.
"I guess I will surprise my mother," Nora said. "She
has a place along here, somewhere."
Nora laughed as if her laugh surprised her. "She has
a turkey farm," she said.
That "somewhere" puzzled Iris, who then caught herself
keeping an eye out in the dark

For a likely place. The moon, growing fatter as it slowly
    eased to westward,
Might show a sideroad or the headlights catch a sign. But
    there was no such place, she knew—
Or thought she knew. "It's set among some redwoods,"
    Nora said. "There were three of us once.
My sister Lolly, me, and Mother. Mother was a stern
    proprietress; business
Was all she cared about. We had the turkeys, a little
    store that served the ranchers,
And because the road to Monterey went past, we had a
    gas pump. Had a father, too.
I've only heard of him. He was a cowboy Mother tamed,
    and died when I was born.
That winter a thermometer had failed and killed a slew
    of hatchlings. He had to go
To Monterey to buy a hundred flats of baby turkeys.
    Driving back—I guess
That he was drunk—he turned into a ditch and broke his
    neck. He missed a cliff, thank God,
As Mother said, and spared the hatchlings and our business.
    That was Mother's consolation."
Nora paused. Iris, worried she would lose her now that
    she'd begun, nearly spoke
But didn't need to. It was only a pause to listen to
    the past. Nora laughed again and said,
"And it consoled her. Lolly watched the turkeys, fed
    them, herded them out of the rain.
You know a turkey's dumb enough to drown in rain. Lolly
    was only a bit smarter.
She had a split inside her you could read in her face.
    She was two people, but we lived with that.

I helped my mother in the store and kept an eye on Lolly.
    It wasn't very lonely."
And then—she couldn't help it—Iris saw her poet studying
    the women—the three
Isolated in their stand of redwoods, with the lonely
    string of road to Monterey
And, back into the mountains, battered paths the ranchers
    came down, even lonelier,
Needing supplies and human company, knowing these women
    and respecting them.
Until the one, lean and out of work, came. He would
    convince the mother she could use him.
He would regard the mad girl sidelong and romance the other
    daughter, slyly letting
The mother fall in love with him as well—his scent, his
    brisk, fluid movements, his body.
Iris could see how it would all be written down, to show
    the things humanity
Could do, even inside a church of giant trees, hearing
    the great sermon of the sea.
How the man would want the mad girl—not the others—
    gobbling among her turkeys, made beautiful
By madness and the grandeur of the place and the absurdity
    of the bird flock.
She had to stop him. She had to stop herself. And heard
    Nora repeat, "I had to get away."
Of course. And Iris knew she had to listen, to look
    before her at the fan of headlights
And glance beside her at the stranger talking about her
    life. To stay awake, she had
To do these things. And leave her poet circling high
    above, his vision like a star,

Blazing with patient disinterest, as the humans, far
    below, threw forth their feeble beams
And followed them along the moonlit coast. To listen to
    another is a kind
Of discipline. Her own tale, if it was worth the telling,
    would wait—if not, she would forget it.
"I'd walk up in the hills behind our place," Nora was
    saying, "and find a ridge and sit
And look out at the ocean. It was like visiting someone
    sick in bed. From there,
The ocean made no sound and had a sleepy look, remote and
    unimpressed by kindness.
I never got away for long. I'd take an hour or less.
    Climbing and coming down
Took all the time. Then, back to Mother working on the
    books and Lolly with the turkeys.
You'd think that she was practicing to imitate them, the
    way she listened and replied.
She was believable. She knew they gobbled in response
    to other sounds—a crow
Or blue jay crying or the whinny of a rancher's horse
    or a car going by."
Nora screamed like a blue jay, then she answered with a
    bubbling gabble from her throat.
Iris gasped and said, "You scared me!" Nora went on,
    "It was boring or entertaining. It depended.
And finally I had to get away. I came down from the ridge
    south of our place,
One day, and found the road and waited for a car. The
    morning overcast hung on
And that meant rain. I don't know why I didn't cross
    the road and hitchhike south. I stayed

On my side, like a child, and wondered which would come
    first—rain or car. Between the trees,
The ocean watched me, winking gray and white. It knew
    what I was up to. If I cocked
My head just so I made it nod and promise to say nothing.
    I didn't do a thing;
A car stopped. There was a woman driving—just like you."
    Iris smiled and looked at her,
But Nora stared ahead and lit a cigarette; the match glow
    showed her thoughtfulness.
"She asked where I was going and I told her I'd go as far
    as *she* went; that bothered her.
The rain began and she looked over at me as if I'd made
    it start. Her tires were bad,
She said. She'd have to stop until the rain let up. Rain
    like that could last for days,
I told her. Then, what should come up on our right?
    She pulled in to our place, before the pump."
Iris began to laugh. "You think that's funny?" Nora
    said. "End of adventure.
She said she'd wait the rain out here. So, I said come
    on in and meet my family.
'Mother, somebody's here,' I said. And Mother told me
    quick to go help Lolly with the turkeys.
I told you how they'd drown themselves in rain. They
    open their dumb throats like drainpipes
And sluice the water down into their lungs. My mother
    told the woman what I'd told her—
That rain like this could last a day or more. I left
    them talking about a room for the night.
But thought about the way they looked together. My
    mother is a small, plump, shapeless woman.

I'm like her, as you've noticed. This other woman stood
    a head above her, like a hat tree.
I found my sister Lolly in the yard, standing among the
    turkeys, gulping down rain.
Some birds already shuddered on their sides, half drowned:
    the others stood transfixed, like her—
Mouths open to the downpour. They were young birds, a
    flock that we were raising for Thanksgiving.
The yard churned and detonated in the rain, pink mud and
    turkey shit and feed and feathers.
The first thing that I had to do was shoo the birds in.
    I grabbed some by the feet and made
A gobbling bouquet of turkey flowers. We lost about
    a dozen birds. I screamed at Lolly
The whole time, screamed and swore and told her what
    I'd do when I was finished. She was deaf.
The rain came down so hard, hammering the yard, the
    tin roofs of the turkey sheds, our skin.
But it felt good to scream. I went for Lolly. I meant
    to shoo her in, too, like a turkey,
But she clung to a fence post. I pulled her and pulled
    off her wet jeans—she was so thin—
And lost my footing. We both slipped in the mud.
    Lolly wiggled away and I came after,
Both of us smeared with pink clay mud, slippery as
    salamanders. She held on and I climbed her.
The rain rinsed us and the mud stuck us together. The
    turkeys bobbed their heads and when we screamed,
They gobbled in response, watching from the sheds.
    Really, the sounds all washed together—
Our screams, the turkeys' chanting, and the rain. I
    had my fingertips on Lolly's, prying

Away her grip, when Mother touched my hands. She stood
    above us, trying to separate us.
She didn't want to fall down in the mud, though she was
    soaked with rain, too; didn't want
To get her hands all muddy, though she saw I needed
    help. Lolly flipped on her back,
Cut our mother's feet from underneath her, and squirmed
    away. Mother looked at her hands
And muddy jeans and shook her head at me—two tubby women
    sitting in pink mud,
Who'd tried to fight a witch become an eel. Lolly
    climbed the fence and disappeared—
I saw her turn the corner to the store front. I helped
    my mother to her feet. I slogged
To the gate. Mother retrieved the jeans I'd pulled off
    Lolly. I watched her fold them in a daze,
But then I hurried after my mad sister. I saw her
    pounding on the strange woman's car door.
The woman was in the car—it looked like she was leaving—
    and there was this pink muddy creature
Pounding to be let in and another in pursuit! She let
    her in—I don't know why—
And Lolly locked the door and looked at me and grinned.
    I rapped the window. I shouted. I implored
Them both to let me in. When Lolly saw the woman wasn't
    leaving, she grabbed the dashboard,
As if she could push and pull the car away inside. I
    heard her screaming at the woman
Who now was looking out at me imploringly. I pointed
    at the button-lock.
Now, what was strange was that the rain was easing up,
    and underneath the clouds the sun,

Starting towards the horizon, sent an orange glow that
    lit the falling drops. It caught
Everybody's attention—it was so sudden and unexpected.
    My sister saw the light,
Coming behind her, reflected in the windows of the store.
    The woman at the wheel
Reached over quickly and undid the lock. I jerked the
    door open—Mother was helping now—
And we grabbed Lolly. We pulled and the woman pushed
    her out. Her muddy legs and hands left smears
Across the dashboard and upholstery. You could see the
    horror on that woman's face
Wasn't just for the madness of it all, with Lolly
    screaming, 'Bitches!' and the three of us
Like mud wrestlers. Partly it was the mess inside her
    car. We started dragging Lolly
Toward the front door. She'd made herself go rigid.
    Mother and I each had her by a foot.
That light still streamed in underneath the clouds. The
    rain drops looked like beads of it. The mud,
A sickening pink, turned rosy and smooth with gleaming
    silver streaks. The woman started her car.
Lolly stopped screaming. Mother and I stopped dragging.
    We all watched—Lolly on her stomach, our grip
On her legs loosening. The woman glanced at us, without
    remorse, still looking as she had
When we pulled Lolly from her car. She backed around,
    stopped, nearly couldn't get traction, spun
Mud in two rooster tails that missed us—though it wouldn't
    have mattered—and then was gone, on her bad tires.
The rain was almost over, so I guess she thought it was
    safe. But we sort of died. Even Lolly relaxed

And stood up on her own. It hurt our feelings to see
   that woman was afraid of us."

Iris drew a breath that filled her up; a long com-
   miserating sigh came out.
The moon, rotund and slow, sent out a sleeker image
   across the hill of water. Without it,
With only starlight, what would be out there? Simply
   an absence that they drove along.
They had passed San Simeon, Big Sur, crawling through
   night, listening to each other. Enough—
Their company had been enough, though darkness helped.
   The resonance of Nora's pain—
To be someone to fear!—lingered. Nora lit a cigarette.
   "When I left, at last,"
She said, turning her face to look past Iris at the sinking
   moon, "it was no big deal.
I asked my mother for money for a trip to San Francisco.
   Thanksgiving had come and gone.
It was our down time. I told myself I'd find that woman
   who fled from us. I never went back.
And never found her. I've kept to this route, working
   here and there, living with people, always
Planning to come home some day." Iris had to interrupt.
   "Is it some place nearby
Or have we passed it?" The coastal road curved inland,
   descended, lights appeared. It was near midnight.
This had to be Carmel, and Nora answered, "No. It's here.
   We're here." Then, Iris said,
"I mean your mother's place. Have we gone by it or is
   it still ahead?"

Nora rolled down her window and let the night stream in,
    its humid wind, lights
Of edge-of-town gas stations, coffee shops. She tossed
    her cigarette into that night.
"I wouldn't tell a soul," she said. "When I go back,
    I'll go alone." Iris felt tired.
It had to be enough that Nora answered, spoke to her
    and not herself. She said,
"Let's stop for coffee. Hungry?" Nora said nothing;
    retracted, like a sea anemone,
She made herself a dark lump in the corner. Iris saw
    a place, a coffee shop.
"I have to eat," she said. "And then I have to sleep.
    And then I'm going to visit Tor House."
She said it as a declaration and an invitation. When
    she parked the car,
She didn't ask if Nora would come with her. She opened
    her door, locked it, as she would,
Knowing a companion would come with her. She paused,
    though, at the entrance, looking back.
The parking lot light made an underworld of daytime
    below the towering night,
And just beyond the road, the valley opened; huge trees
    the light just reached, ascending shapes
Of deep opacity, stood waiting. But not for Iris, not
    for Nora, though Iris waited.
And, so it seemed to Iris, Nora waited—for obstinacy
    to pass, or fear.
Was this the valley Jeffers said Orion rose from in
    December, strung across its throat
Like a bridge of lights? The trees—she saw the silhouettes
    of eucalyptus—obscured the view

Of any stars climbing out of the valley. The car door
   opened, shut. She watched
As Nora walked toward her, the floppy stetson pulled
   down on her head, the khaki coat
Hugged tight. Yes, it was cool, damp, with the closeness
   of dense trees and ocean. Iris felt it,
Even standing in the overlit bleak parking lot of an
   all night coffee shop.
She smiled but Nora looked down, then entered the restaurant
   with her, keeping a touching-distance
Like a shadow or a child. She came to Iris's shoulder.
   Iris did a doubletake.
"I'm not that tall, am I?" she asked herself and was
   happy when the contrast disappeared,
Sitting at a booth. "It's exciting just to be here,"
   Iris said. And, at once,
Felt foolish. Nora looked at her, took off her hat as
   if to doff it to a lady,
And set it on the seat beside her. She lit up and the
   smoke gave her an air of understanding.
They ordered coffee. Iris had been hungry. Now, looking
   at Nora clearly, across from her,
Her face lined by the years of smoking, the eyes olive-
   drab, attentive, she seemed older.
Though Iris had felt older in the car, she saw that
   Nora was her age.
Her hands with their fat fingers showed veins, creases.
   Looking at his attentive woman, waiting
For Iris to say something, to talk to her, the appetite
   was gone, the hunger gone.
And in its place a rushing flow of need, like juices in
   the mouth and belly, another

Hunger. Iris remembered her description of the woman's
    picture, behind the door
For years, discovered in her fantasy by her poet and his
    wife. A door swung shut.
Iris was the one behind the door. Discovered, she could
    speak. The door swung shut on decades,
Generations, all the past. And she could speak of it.
    Nora could study her.
She saw that Nora's curiosity was like her own, but she
    was not a painting
To be imagined into life. "When I think how I grew up
    in Kentucky," she began,
"It breaks my heart. We had to live wherever Mama found
    to live, my two brothers and me,
After our daddy died. With men who rented land and farmed
    it. Men she met in bars
And other places. Now, I see she was resourceful,
    resilient, too. She'd find a man,
Bind him to her, then introduce her children to the bargain.
    My brothers learned to farm.
My mother saved. She worked to keep us growing up. I
    think that was her calling.
When I was old enough for college and my brothers had
    some acreage of their own, Mama
Let herself go a little. Her resilience turned to
    hardness, resourcefulness to greed.
But that's a theory. Unfair probably. Based on coming
    home from a bad marriage.
In college I got pregnant. I took an English class
    that studied Robinson Jeffers.
Nine girls and one shy boy, besides the teacher. I fell
    in love with Jeffers, with the teacher,

And, because he asked me questions after class, and
   always looked dazed
When I responded—as if I were a prom queen or a picture
   in a magazine—
I fell for that shy boy. When I think back, I wonder why
   we studied Jeffers there,
Along with others. He was the teacher's favorite. He
   made the place we lived seem insufficient.
Western Kentucky isn't very grand. But I began an argument
   with him—
The poet—about my life. I couldn't have explained it to
   you, then. Then, I was falling
In love because I was loved; going to bed with Cale,
   getting pregnant. My argument
Was notions that would flash like images, contrasting
   with things that Jeffers said
About people, animals, places—people, animals, places
   I had never seen. I left school
To marry Cale. He wanted to get out and start a business,
   down where he was from,
In Tennessee. The first night of our honeymoon, in
   Nashville, he punched me in the back.
A real wallop! I was standing by the bed, getting
   dressed. I was surprised.
It seemed I wasn't hurrying. He looked dazed when I
   turned to him, but not with admiration,
The way he used to when I'd let him ask me questions
   after class. It took four years
For me to understand I was in danger. I left with
   bruises on my face and ribs
And took my little girl—our daughter Ruth—back home
   to Mama and my brothers." Iris felt

A swelling and contracting in her skull. Nora regarded
    her with a doctor's calm,
Having heard nothing yet to make a note of. But Iris
    thought, "Don't tell her everything!"
"Well, I had other reasons, too," said Iris, studying
    Nora's face for irony.
Nothing—the scrim of smoke, the coffee cup ascending to
    the lips, the listener's eyes.
"That summer back at home—I won't lie to you—I can think
    of in two ways. The first—
I kept house for my brothers; they were good uncles to
    their niece and babysat her evenings
When I went into town to the college library. My mother
    had become a drunk
But had a manfriend, no older than her sons, who kept
    her occupied. He gardened for us.
We all had things to do. Looking back the first way,
    I can see an order—
Me cooking, my brothers farming, Ruth catching frogs
    along the sandy creek beds where they fished,
Mama coming home drunk weekend nights, her friend tending
    the peppers and tomatoes
And helping her to bed. I even got some consolation
    after Cale.
I met the teacher who had taught me Jeffers, met him
    in the library. I got to talk
About my poet with somebody who understood—not that
    I said Jeffers was
My poet; I kept that secret. But other things I thought
    I understood. We slept together.
Then, things went wrong. That's the second way of looking
    back. Just all the sudden things

Went wrong. I came home from the grocery store one day,
    with Ruth, my little girl, and found them—
My brothers, Mama's friend, and Mama—bound and face down,
    shotgunned in the head. My child
Saw that. Mama managed to survive, but wouldn't—couldn't—
    speak. She was a blank.
Hard to believe my story takes this turn. Things go along
    in family life just fine,
Then, all the sudden it comes to an end. But that's not
    all the truth here. They had raised
A crop of marijuana. They had done it once before success-
    fully—my brothers
And my mother—and liked the money. I was convinced that
    being home with danger growing
In the drainage ditches hidden by the corn was safer
    for my daughter and me.
It almost has the tragic size that Jeffers liked, doesn't
    it? But I remember
Comedy. Sad comedy. Two rabid foxes bit our little
    wiener dog; we panicked;
Killed him. My teacher/lover took me and my daughter in,
    then wouldn't touch me. Finally,
When Mama was as well as she was going to get, I put us
    all—her, me, and Ruth—
Into our truck and drove to California. I meant to make
    it here, but ended up
Three hundred miles south for twenty years." Iris tried
    to smile, to make her listener
Smile, too, but Nora hid her mouth behind her hand. In
    thoughtfulness? The eyes said so.
If Nora had looked horrified, Iris could calm her,
    say the comedy

Was how they had survived. Despite absurdity and horror,
   they had made it through.
"You wonder how I managed to remain in one place twenty
   years? I have to guess.
It was the peace of nothing happening that made me want
   to stay there. Once I could tell
That nothing drastic would occur, I got like Mama. My
   mama watched TV all day.
My way of watching was to see my Ruth grow up, in sunshine,
   under palms, become
No different from other creatures in that paradise.
   Happy and not so smart
That she would ever suffer discontentment and want to leave.
   We silently agreed
We had no past beyond the day that we discovered California.
   Besides,
I wanted to erase what she had seen and in the process
   cancel out her father.
I think that I succeeded. She's married now. Her husband
   needs her. She won't go anywhere.
And Mama's dead. And the man—I guess I ought to mention
   him—I've left the man I lived with.
I did what Mama used to do. Got hold of someone to take
   care of us and held on.
She never lasted with a man as I did, as I swore I would.
   We had a life.
It happened as an accident but it wasn't just convenience.
   I might have helped him
More quickly to his grave than if he'd never met me, or
   I might have slowed him down.
I feel responsible yet free as well. You'd think with
   all the death in it, my life

Would be a tragedy. But I've kept my real life a secret—
    reading Jeffers
And trying to imagine him imagining someone like me. It's
    when he says
He has been saved from human illusion and foolishness
    and passion and wants to be like rock
That I miss something. I think I have been steadfast,
    but what does rock feel? I like him in bereavement—
When saying man can't last long, then admitting, since
    his wife's death, that he is short of patience.
Wanting to die, to lay his body down where he has found
    the wounded deer have done so,
In the hidden clearing on the cliff edge, then refusing
    to. That's when I like to read him.
Una is the woman I believe most in his poems. Even when
    she's gone.
My God, I'm hungry!" Iris laughed at her own statement.
    Nora jerked her head back
And made as if to leave. "No, no," said Iris. "I was
    hungry when we came in here,
And now I'm going to eat. Let's both eat. It's on me.
    Don't leave." Nora had lost the pose
Of calm detachment and attention and begun to close again,
    to furl up.
But Iris ordered for them both—pancakes and bacon—and
    they both, two hungry women, ate.

To raise a stump of rock into a tower, rolling a stone
    in place as the years pass.
Strangers who only know your silhouette bid it farewell
    and travel to Japan,

Cross China, venture into India, to Europe, and, changed
  by time and space,
Sail home over the bulging eye of ocean only to see, when
  landfall looms in view,
The stump of rock—your tower—on the headland, and you
  there, rolling a stone in place,
The edifice apparently no taller, as if each night you
  had dismantled it
And every day had raised it up again. To know, only in
  completion, the nisus
That dominates the spider when it spins, the bird building
  its nest, the gray whale
Turning toward Mexico and the sea lion clambering up shingle
  toward its mate—
The nisus of cairn-building, rock-piling, mortaring stone
  has dominated you.
It dominates the reader bent above the book, poised like
  a stork hunting; like sleep,
It is an utter unity of will and action, known—at least
  by man or woman—
Only when it is over. And when the work is over—tower
  building, poem writing—
You hear gulls cry and see them kiting at the bull terrier
  out in the garden.
He has snatched up some strip of bloody fur they meant to
  mince with beaks. Best to detach it
From his jaws, let gulls eat refuse like that. Go out
  into the damp twilight, feel
The chill along the arms, through cloth, and take the
  petty morsel from the pet dog, toss it
To the scolding gulls, down the rocky bank beyond the
  garden. And lead the dog to food

Inside the kitchen. Enter, expecting to see the woman,
     the two sons, and your place at table,
Waiting. And find you are alone. Even the dog at heel—
     vanished. The stone house
Glumly dark and a dumb cold coming from its walls, that
     only whiskey cuts.
The cold and dark conceal much, and memory must be evoked
     to penetrate them.
Meanwhile, they are the elements that starlight loves.
     Clear cold, pure darkness, outside the window,
Beside the guestbed, where you have planned to lie at
     last, viewing the pure, clear stars without
Obstruction by the crude suburban dwellings—that absurd
     roof, down there, like a coal scoop,
And the spite fences either side your property. Nothing
     in creation shows
More the supreme indifference to humanity, despite the
     patterns of the zodiac.
The stars, like bits of crystal ground into a grist-
     stone's granite rim, are small themselves.
Only the surrounding emptiness is great. Take comfort
     in the emptiness; lie down.
The drink will help you sleep awhile alone, without her,
     until that section of the night
You've come to know—that region you once sailed through
     peacefully, worn out by work and love.
Now, stranded there till dawn, sleepless, it will not
     matter that you foresaw the planet's end
Or our end on the planet. Only sleep will matter. At
     that hour, in those conditions,
Just out of reach, receding like the dark itself as day-
     light pushes in, sleep only

Will be the thing you want. Powerless to attain what
    you desire, yet bitterly
Desiring at all costs. Perhaps, then, memory, not star-
    light, will intercede,
And the stone house gather warmth from its hearth fire,
    and loved ones reappear, and you will sleep.

When both had eaten it was three a.m. Two young men
    at the counter teased the waitress.
Another couple, Iris saw, much like Nora and herself, had
    ordered breakfast.
In such a place the night meant only a thinner crowd,
    fewer faces looking back
From the reflective windows. Beyond that, the usual
    business and the accustomed feeling
That daytime was your night. "Do you think we can find
    a place?" asked Iris. Nora echoed
The question in her voice, "*The* place?" Iris could
    tell that they had puzzled one another.
"I mean a place to sleep," said Iris. "I'll put you up
    if you need money. I'll take you home,
If you will let me in the morning, if you will tell me
    where you live." "I live with you,"
Said Nora. Now Iris pulled back and looked for an escape;
    crisscrossing inner voices said,
"She doesn't mean it. If she does, what then? She's
    crazy. She is not. Try to help her."
Iris saw Nora crack a smile—clairvoyant in its mockery.
    "Calm down," Nora said,
Again dispassionate, taking once again the adult role
    from Iris, sadly

Acknowledging by her tone that Iris feared her. "I'll
   show you where we both can sleep, and then
We'll see," said Nora. "We'll see when we wake up."
   Nora directed Iris up the highway,
Then left into the cramped expensive neighborhoods of
   Carmel. Amber porch lights cut
The outlines of concealing garden shrubbery, wadded
   between front door and street.
Another left. Parked cars narrowed the road. Iris
   maneuvered down its middle slowly
As if half drunk, waiting for Nora's quiet indication.
   "Now, left again."
Ahead was the vast night of the ocean at Carmel Bay.
   No light there. But as they turned
They heard it beyond the veil of street lights, the lit
   stretch of rocky-sand—the *Yes*
Of waves arriving ceaselessly. *Yes*, then, the soft
   collapse, *We've come, We've come.*
Nora again directed, "Left here. Careful now. Look
   for a place to park." The street
Tilted slightly as if climbing the back of a low hill.
   Along it, houses crowded—
That close California-greed for space, even among
   mansions. "Here," said Nora.
Iris pulled over to the right and stopped. Her headlights,
   before she turned them off, showed her
The trunks of cypresses, along the street. She'd parked
   below one and rolled her window down.
She heard its canopy stirring in the onshore breezes, or
   thought she did. Coast cypresses.
His trees. Nora unlatched her seat and leaned it back.
   "Nobody would think," she said,

"A couple of homeless women would just park here for the
   night." But Iris heard the trees
And the voice that she'd made up for him, saying, "If
   you should look for this place after a handful of lifetimes,
Perhaps of my planted forest a few may stand yet." She
   grabbed the door handle; she had to see it,
Even in the dark. Nora stopped her with a touch. "Let's
   sleep now. Don't wake up his neighbors."
Iris settled back. Up through the windshield she thought
   she could perceive the cypress branches
Interlocking with a wheel of stars. As she fell asleep,
   she heard herself and Nora
Saying Jeffers' poems back and forth. In fact, they
   both said nothing, but held hands.

Iris woke up under the gaze of strangers—Nora's eyes
   as she began to light
A morning cigarette, still lying back; when she saw Iris
   wake she smiled and gestured.
And, peering into the car, the eyes of a man and woman
   weeding a patch of ivy; they bent
To pluck out stalks of oatgrass while looking at the women
   stirring in this parked car. The man,
Brown-skinned in gray workclothes, tried not to look too
   much. But the woman seemed about to speak.
Her clothes were brighter yellow than the sunshine,
   coming full tilt now through the windshield,
Her lips and sunglass rims a purple-red like bougainvillea,
   under a straw hat.
Iris checked her watch—past ten a. m. And now she saw
   the simple mail box—*Jeffers*

In white letters. Iris and Nora brought their seats erect,
   got out, and said together,
"We've come to take the tour." Iris tried to give herself
   a subdued stretch and, instead,
Quivered like a bowstring. The woman in the yellow sunsuit
   turned away.
Nora stretched, too, her plump midriff shaking, and looked
   up toward the sun. She read it full-face,
Pushing her stetson back, her round, plain face made beautiful,
   as Iris saw it, because
It held the sunshine streaming through the cypresses, roundly,
   plainly. The street was lined
With evergreens, adult trees, the remnants of his forest
   tailored to a residential street.
Without the sculpted windward sweep of their wild cousins
   on the cliffs, these trees looked ready
For some test that would clear all houses from their feet—
   all but his alone—and leave them standing.
Iris and Nora walked to the house gate. The sky came down
   behind the tower, pale blue
And almost white along the seam it made with ocean. The
   sky the water was reflecting,
Iris thought, could not be that sky. It had to be some
   wine dark, purple sky, or cloth,
Bleeding a blue dye underneath its surface. But what she
   could not bear at first was how close
It all was. A few strides would let her lay her hand on
   the square tower. Its angles made
Of boulders he had set, each rounded to a softness, though
   heavy with mass, dense with weight.
And the stone house equally in reach. She felt the power
   to say, but only to herself,

She knew reality because it looked her in the face. Nothing
    could duplicate
The face-to-face regard of something real. Nora held
    the gate for her. The docent,
Waiting to begin her tour, welcomed them to join two older
    men.
The men were looking at the pathway to the house. Among
    the cobblestones, a green tile,
Marked with a wave pattern, had been laid. These personal
    touches, said the guide, were everywhere.
The garden filled the space between the house and tower.
    An English garden, Una's work.
In answer to a question from the older of the men, the guide
    said yes, he'd built
A secret passage in the tower for his sons. They'd see it
    last. And climb the tower.
Iris held back a little as the party entered the small house.
    In the side garden,
In the full sunlight sweeping Carmel Bay from here to Point
    Lobos, a line of iris stood,
Robust, two feet tall, their long petals curling back,
    lavender, blue, and deep red-purple—
The ocean's color. Yes. She felt a secret lodge with
    her, to keep, and entered the low door,
The house where pain and pleasure had turned to poetry
    and stone, and a family had been happy.